Editor
Heather Douglas

Managing Editor
Ina Massler Levin, M.A.

Cover Artist
Brenda DiAntonis

Art Production Manager
Kevin Barnes

Imaging
James Edward Grace
Ricardo Martinez

Publisher
Mary D. Smith, M.S. Ed.

MASTERING
FOURTH GRADE
SKILLS

Author

Teacher Created Resources Staff

Teacher Created Resources

Teacher Created Resources, Inc.
6421 Industry Way
Westminster, CA 92683
www.teachercreated.com
ISBN-1-4206-3943-9
©2006 Teacher Created Resources, Inc.
Made in U.S.A.

Table of Contents

Introduction

The wealth of knowledge a person gains throughout his or her lifetime is impossible to measure, and it will certainly vary from person to person. However, regardless of the scope of knowledge, the foundation for all learning remains a constant. All that we know and think throughout our lifetimes is based upon fundamentals, and these fundamentals are the basic skills upon which all learning develops. *Mastering Fourth Grade Skills* is a book that reinforces a variety of fourth grade basic skills.

- **Writing**
- **Grammar**
- **Literature**
- **Math**
- **Social Studies**
- **Science**

This book was written with the wide range of student skills and ability levels of fourth grade students in mind. Both teachers and parents can benefit from the variety of pages provided in this book. Parents can use the book to provide an introduction to new material or to reinforce material already familiar to their children. Similarly, teachers can select pages that provide additional practice for concepts taught in the classroom. When tied to what is being covered in class, pages from this book make great homework reinforcement. The worksheets provided in this book are ideal for use at home as well as in the classroom. Research shows us that skill mastery comes with exposure and drill. To be internalized, concepts must be reviewed until they become second nature. Parents may certainly foster the classroom experience by exposing their children to the necessary skills whenever possible, and teachers will find that these pages perfectly complement their classroom needs. An answer key, beginning on page 231, provides teachers, parents, and children with a quick method of checking responses to completed worksheets.

Basic skills are utilized every day in untold ways. Make the practice of them part of your children's or students' routines. Such work done now will benefit them in countless ways throughout their lives.

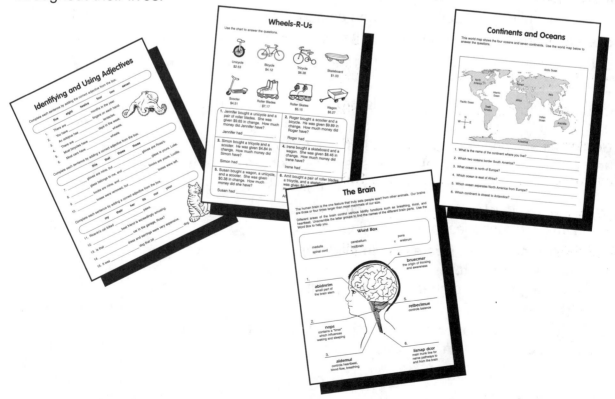

Meeting Standards

Each lesson in *Mastering Fourth Grade Skills* meets one or more of the following standards, which are used with permission from McREL (Copyright 2000, McREL, Mid-continent Research for Education and Learning. Telephone: 303-337-0990. Website: *www.mcrel.org*).

Standard	Page Number
Language Arts:	
Uses the general skills and strategies of the writing process	
• Uses prewriting strategies to plan written work	78, 91–96
• Uses strategies to draft and revise written work	78–82
• Uses strategies to edit and publish written work	82–83
• Uses strategies to write for a variety of purposes	84–88, 97
Uses the stylistic and rhetorical aspects of writing	
• Uses descriptive language that clarifies and enhances ideas	72–74, 76
• Uses paragraph form in writing	77,84–91,97
• Uses a variety of sentence structures in writing	20–21,66–71,79
Uses grammatical and mechanical conventions in written compositions	
• Uses exclamatory and imperative sentences in written compositions	20–21
• Uses nouns in written compositions	8
• Uses verbs in written compositions	10
• Uses adjectives in written compositions	9
• Uses adverbs in written compositions	11
• Uses conjunctions in written compositions	12
• Uses conventions of spelling in written compositions	82, 84–88, 97
• Uses conventions of capitalization in written compositions	13–14
• Uses conventions of punctuation in written compositions	15–21
Uses the general skills and strategies of the reading process	
• Makes, confirms, and revises simple predictions about what will be found in a text	42–43
• Uses phonetic and structural analysis techniques to decode unknown words (e.g., vowel patterns, syllabication, root words, affixes)	22–31, 34–35
• Uses a variety of context clues to decode unknown words	37–38
• Understands level-appropriate reading vocabulary (e.g., synonyms, antonyms, homophones, multi-meaning words)	32–33, 36
Uses reading skills and strategies to understand a variety of literary passages and texts	
• Uses reading skills and strategies to understand a variety of literary passages and texts	46–48, 51–65
• Understands basic concept of plot (e.g., main problem, conflict, resolution, cause-and-effect)	39–41, 46–48

Meeting Standards (cont.)

Standard	Page Number
Language Arts: (cont.)	
• Understands similarities and differences within and among literary works from various genre and cultures	47–65
• Makes inferences or draws conclusions about characters' qualities and actions	44–45
• Understands the ways in which language is used in literary texts (e.g., personification, simile, metaphor, imagery, rhythm)	75
Uses reading skills and strategies to understand and interpret a variety of informational texts	
• Uses reading skills and strategies to understand a variety of informational texts	49–50, 59–65
Math:	
Understands and applies basic and advanced properties of the concepts of numbers	
• Understands equivalent forms of basic percents, fractions, and decimals	138
• Understands the relative magnitude and relationships among whole numbers, fractions, decimals, and mixed numbers	133–139, 143–144, 146
Uses basic and advanced procedures while performing the processes of computation	
• Adds, subtracts, multiplies, and divides whole numbers and decimals	98–132
• Adds and subtracts simple fractions	140–142, 145, 147
Understands and applies basic and advanced properties of the concepts of measurement	
• Understands the basic measures perimeter, area, volume, capacity, mass, angle, and circumference	161–167
Understands and applies basic and advanced properties of the concepts of geometry	
• Knows basic geometric language for describing and naming shapes (e.g., trapezoid, parallelogram, cube, sphere)	148–151
• Understands basic properties of figures (e.g., two- or three-dimensionality, symmetry, number of faces, type of angle)	150, 152–153, 155–158
• Understands that shapes can be congruent or similar	154, 158
• Uses motion geometry (e.g., turns, flips, slides) to understand geometric relationships	168–169
• Understands characteristics of lines (e.g., parallel, perpendicular, intersecting) and angles (e.g., right, acute)	156–157, 159–160

Meeting Standards *(cont.)*

Standard	Page Number
Math: *(cont.)* **Understands and applies basic and advanced concepts of statistics and data analysis**	
• Organizes and displays data in simple bar graphs, pie charts, and line graphs	144, 170–186
• Understands that data come in many different forms and that collecting, organizing, and displaying data can be done in many ways	170–186
Social Studies/Geography: **Understands the history of a local community and how communities in North America varied long ago**	
• Knows geographical settings, economic activities, food, clothing, homes, crafts, and rituals of Native American societies long ago (e.g., Iroquois, Sioux, Hopi, Nez Perce, Inuit, Cherokee)	187–191, 208
Understands the people, events, problems, and ideas that were significant in creating the history of their stay	
• Understands geographic, economic, and religious reasons that brought the first explorers and settlers to the state or region, who they were, and where they settled	192
Understands how democratic values came to be, and how they have been exemplified by people, events, and symbols	
• Knows the Pledge of Allegiance and patriotic songs, poems, and sayings that were written long ago, and understands their significance	193–195
Understands selected attributes and historical developments of societies in Africa, the Americas, Asia, and Europe	
• Knows about the migrations of large groups in the past and recently	196–197
• Knows about European explorers of the 15th and 16th centuries, their reasons of exploring, the information gained from their journeys, and what happened as a result of their travels	198
Understands the characteristics and uses of maps, globes, and other geographic tools and technologies	
• Knows the basic elements of maps and globes	199–201, 205–210
• Uses map grids	202–203, 207
Knows the location of places, geographical features, and patterns of the environment	
• Knows the approximate location of continents, major mountain ranges, and bodies of water on Earth	203–204

Meeting Standards *(cont.)*

Standard	Page Number
Science/Health:	
Understands essential concepts about nutrition and diet	
• Knows the nutritional value of different foods	216
• Knows healthy eating practices (e.g., eating a nutritious breakfast, eating a variety of foods, eating nutritious meals and snacks at regular intervals to satisfy individual energy and growth needs	211–215
Knows how to maintain and promote personal health	
• Knows the basic structure and functions of the human body systems (e.g., how they are interrelated)	217–218
Understands atmospheric processes and the water cycle	
• Knows that water exists in the air in different forms (e.g., in clouds and fog as tiny droplets; in rain, snow, and hail) and changes from one form to another through various processes (e.g., freezing, condensation, precipitation, evaporation)	225–226
Understands Earth's composition and structure	
• Knows how features on the Earth's surface are constantly changed by a combination of slow and rapid processes (e.g., weathering, erosion, transport, and deposition of sediment caused by waves, wind, water, and ice; landslides, volcanic eruptions, earthquakes, drought)	219–222
Understands the composition and structure of the universe and the earth's place in it	
• Knows that the Earth is one of several planets that orbit the Sun and that the Moon orbits the Earth	227–228
Understands relationships among organisms and their physical environment	
• Knows that all organisms (including humans) cause changes in their environments, and these changes can be beneficial or detrimental	229
Understands the sources and properties of energy	
• Knows that heat is often produced as a byproduct when one form of energy is converted to another form	223
• Knows the organization of a simple electrical circuit	224
Understands the structure and function of cells and organisms	
• Knows that living organisms have distinct structures and body systems that serve specific functions in growth, survival, and reproduction	230

Identifying Common and Proper Nouns

A noun is a word that names something.

Common nouns name general people, places, or things.

Proper nouns name specific people, places, or things.

Use the lines before each word to label the following nouns **C** for common nouns or **P** for proper nouns. On the lines after the nouns, write a matching proper noun after each common noun and a matching common noun after each proper noun.

Examples: 1. ___P___ Asia _____continent_____

2. ___C___ continent _____Antarctica_____

1. _____ England _____
2. _____ day _____
3. _____ month _____
4. _____ Monday _____
5. _____ April _____
6. _____ Venus _____
7. _____ Chicago _____
8. _____ France _____
9. _____ Mother's Day _____
10. _____ ocean _____
11. _____ mountain _____
12. _____ country _____
13. _____ Iowa _____
14. _____ Mt. McKinley _____
15. _____ Lake Ontario _____

16. _____ holiday _____
17. _____ city _____
18. _____ island _____
19. _____ dog _____
20. _____ elephant _____
21. _____ Chevrolet _____
22. _____ teacher _____
23. _____ president _____
24. _____ mayor _____
25. _____ planet _____
26. _____ school _____
27. _____ Mrs. Brown _____
28. _____ Granny Smith _____
29. _____ song _____
30. _____ poem _____

Identifying and Using Adjectives

Complete each sentence by adding the correct adjective from the box.

> **five**   **eight**   **twelve**   **four**   **two**   **seven**

1. There are _____ months in the year.
2. You have _____ fingers on each hand.
3. An octopus has _____ tentacles.
4. There are _____ days in the week.
5. Most bicycles have _____ wheels.
6. Most cars have _____ wheels.

Complete each sentence by adding a correct adjective from the box.

> **this**   **that**   **these**   **those**

7. _____ gloves are mine, but _____ gloves are Rosa's.

8. _____ glass belongs to me, and _____ glass is yours, Luke.

9. _____ books are mine, and _____ books are yours, Lucille.

10. _____ boxes were removed, but _____ boxes were left.

Complete each sentence by adding a correct adjective from the box.

> **my**   **their**   **her**   **its**   **our**   **your**

11. Ricardo's cat licked _____ paws.

12. _____ best friend is exceedingly amusing.

13. Is that _____ car in the garage, Rosa?

14. _____ dress and earrings were very expensive.

15. It was _____ dog that bit _____ dog.

Verbs

Some non-action verbs help action verbs to do their work. They work together in a sentence like a team. These non-action verbs are called *helping verbs*.

Example: Children can play many games at the park.

The non-action helping verb is *can*. The action verb is *play*.

The complete verb is *can play*.

Find the helping and action verbs in the sentences below. Use the following list of verbs to help you. Then fill in the blanks at the bottom of the page by writing the helping and action verbs from the sentences in the correct spaces.

Helping Verbs: *am, is, has, are, were, has, have, had, can, will*

Action Verbs: *drink, ridden, pushed, driven, move, pulled, going, ride, seen, go*

1. Lupita will ride her bicycle.
2. An elephant is ridden in India.
3. The scooters were pushed by the parents.
4. An airplane can move quickly.
5. Alex has driven a truck.

6. Sled dogs have pulled the visitors across the snow.
7. We have seen a bear.
8. You will go to school now.
9. Christopher will eat all the ice cream.
10. We will drink all the root beer.

Helping Verbs

1. _____
2. _____
3. _____
4. _____
5. _____
6. _____
7. _____
8. _____
9. _____
10. _____

Action Verbs

1. _____
2. _____
3. _____
4. _____
5. _____
6. _____
7. _____
8. _____
9. _____
10. _____

Identifying and Using Adverbs

Complete each sentence by choosing an adverb from the box.

| out | here | there | near |

1. The supermarket Lucille goes to is not far; in fact, it is quite _____.

2. Our teacher told us to put the extra book _____.

3. The terrible car accident Ricardo was in occurred right _____.

4. Luke came in the back door as we went _____.

Complete each sentence by choosing an adverb from the box. (Hints are provided in the parentheses.)

| often | now | yesterday | soon |

5. Ricardo has missed his piano lesson _____. (**many times**)

6. We are sure Lucy will arrive _____. (**in a short time**)

7. Do not wait for a moment; write your paragraph _____. (**right away**)

8. Ricardo and Luke went swimming _____. (**the day before today**)

Fill in the blanks to show the positive, comparative, and superlative degrees for the following adverbs. The first one has been done for you.

	Positive Degree	Comparative Degree	Superlative Degree
9.	hard	harder	hardest
10.		more softly	
11.			best
12.	easy		
13.		faster	

Using Coordinating Conjunctions

Combine the following pairs of sentences with *or, and,* or *but.* Remember to place a comma before the coordinating conjunction when combining two complete sentences.

1. You can wear your blue jeans. You can wear your black jeans. _____

_____

2. Your white T-shirt fits better. Your red T-shirt is more colorful. _____

_____

3. Do you want yellow patches on your jeans? Do you want pink patches on your jeans?

_____

_____

4. Jillian's T-shirt looks attractive. Jacqueline's jeans are stunning. _____

_____

5. I have three pairs of blue jeans. I want another pair of blue jeans. _____

_____

6. You can wash your old jeans. You can iron your new jeans. _____

_____

7. This white T-shirt is mine. That white T-shirt is yours. _____

_____

8. Let's wear our blue jeans today. Let's wear our red jeans tomorrow. _____

_____

9. My old jeans fit me well. My new jeans do not fit me very well. _____

_____

10. I have washed my new red T-shirt. I have not washed my new blue T-shirt. _____

_____

Capitalization

The following sentences need capitalizitation. Underline each letter three times that should be changed to a capital and write the capital letter above the crossed out letter.

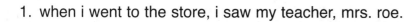

Example: i went to new york on saturday.

1. when i went to the store, i saw my teacher, mrs. roe.

2. my family will go to disneyland in july.

3. i am reading *old yeller* this week.

4. my sister, sarah, says her favorite subject is spanish.

5. on wednesday, we will celebrate groundhog day.

6. my brother said that mom was a cheerleader at eastside high school.

7. in august, we're going to visit aunt mary in san francisco, california.

8. benjie had a birthday, and we sang "happy birthday to you."

9. my friend rosa speaks spanish, and i speak english.

10. my neighbor julia is going to paris, france, next june.

Editing for Capitalization

Directions: Correct errors in capitalization using proofreader's marks.

"Move, David." Standing on the chair, Jonathon reached up to feel the hole. he took his bike lock key out of his pocket and tried it in the keyhole.

"That doesn't come close to fitting," David protested.

Jonathon got off the chair and pushed it back over to the desk. "No," he said, "before I look for a key, I need to know what I'm looking for." He pushed the chair back over to the hole. Then he walked over to the desk, rummaged around, and found a piece of paper and a pencil.

"What are you doing?"

"You'll see." Jonathon climbed back up on the chair, holding the paper and pencil. he had to stand on tiptoe to reach the keyhole; even then, he had to reach up and lean his head back—it was most awkward, but he managed to get a key shape traced.

"Now I'm ready to find the key!" in his enthusiasm, Jonathon forgot about the midday heat.

He ran down the stairs and banged out the screen door. david followed at a more leisurely pace and caught up with Jonathon on the porch.

"Where am I going to look first?" Staring out towards the mulberry tree, jonathon straddled the porch railing and pondered the best place to begin looking for a key. "I know! i'll go down and check around the basement."

"at least it's cool down there," David said.

Separate Day and Year

Use a comma to separate the day and the year from the rest of the sentence. Remember to place a comma after the year when it comes in the middle of a sentence.

1. Jerry was born on October 5 1986.

2. My favorite Christmas was December 25 1992.

3. Susan's mom came home from the hospital on April 6 1994.

4. We took our summer vacation on July 21 1993.

5. My grandfather was born on August 11 1941.

6. On April 6 1994 Susan's mom brought a new baby girl home from the hospital.

7. My grandfather remembers July 20 1969 as an important date in history.

8. On July 21 1993 my family went to Hawaii for our summer vacation.

Using Apostrophes

The apostrophe is used with nouns and indefinite pronouns to show possession. It is also used in contractions to indicate omitted words or letters.

Examples: boy's cap; Luke's cap; men's cap; boys' caps; Jane's cap; girls' caps; one's duty; others' duties; do not, don't; has not, hasn't; she is, she's; it is, it's

Find in each sentence the two words that require apostrophes and write them correctly on the lines.

1. Lukes father said that he couldnt go to my house after school today.

   _____   _____

2. All the Rosas names werent misspelled on the school roster.

   _____   _____

3. Therefore, my friend Rosas name wasnt spelled wrong.

   _____   _____

4. Shell make sure that your name isnt misspelled.

   _____   _____

5. After what Ive been through, itll be nice to have a chance to rest.

   _____   _____

6. My mothers seen to it that her daughters been very busy lately.

   _____   _____

7. Shes kept me working and has even made me do my brothers work.

   _____   _____

8. Thats one of the most unfair things Ive ever had to endure.

   _____   _____

9. I wouldve skipped his chores, but I couldnt get by with doing that.

   _____   _____

10. Its one of lifes most joyous moments when you realize all your work is done.

   _____   _____

11. Doing someone elses work shouldnt be part of my life.

   _____   _____

12. Im told that its not an unusual occurrence, no matter how old you are.

   _____   _____

Using Quotation Marks

Commas are used to set off quotations. Example: She said, "I don't like bananas." The comma after *she said* tells us to pause before speaking the quote. Place the quotation marks and commas where they are needed.

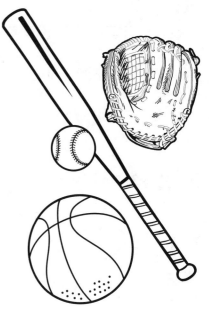

1. Ryan asked What do you want to play, Martha?

2. Martha answered Let's play baseball.

3. Okay, we'll play baseball first said Ryan but let's play basketball after that.

4. Mom called The cookies are ready.

5. Oh, boy they both yelled at the same time let's eat!

Write four sentences below. Make it a conversation between you and your best friend. Be sure to place the quotation marks where they belong.

_____

_____

_____

_____

_____

_____

_____

_____

It's Mine...Or Maybe It's Yours

> **Punctuation Rules:** Use an apostrophe to show ownership. An apostrophe is used to form the possessive case of a singular noun by adding an apostrophe and then the letter *s*.

Write a **C** on the line provided if the apostrophe is used correctly. Write an **X** if the apostrophe is used incorrectly.

_____ 1. dog's bone

_____ 2. deer's antlers

_____ 3. televisions' remote

_____ 4. womans' jacket

_____ 5. book's title

_____ 6. his' football

Change the following singular nouns to singular possessive nouns.

7. cat dish _____

8. dog treat _____

9. teacher desk _____

10. Kayla Beth doll _____

11. horse oats _____

Read over the list of objects. Using an apostrophe, give each object a singular owner.

Example: guitar _____ the musician's guitar _____

12. banjo _____

13. pizza _____

14. notebook _____

15. money _____

Punctuation

Sentences have three kinds of end marks, depending on the kinds of sentences they are. A *declarative* sentence tells something. It has a period at the end. An *interrogative* sentence asks a question. An interrogative sentence has a question mark at the end. An *exclamatory* sentence exclaims, shouts, or yells. An exclamatory sentence has an exclamation point at the end.

Here is an example of each kind.

Declarative Sentence: I decided to relax in the hammock.

Interrogative Sentence: Have you ever slept in a hammock?

Exclamatory Sentence: The hammock broke, and I fell on my dog!

Now it is your turn to use end punctuation. Write the correct punctuation at the end of each sentence. Then write a **D** for declarative, **I** for interrogative, or **E** for exclamatory on the line before each sentence.

_____ 1. Where did you get that hat

_____ 2. Oh, no, the ball's headed this way

_____ 3. It's time to go to school

_____ 4. There's an octopus on your head

_____ 5. Have you seen my pet snake

_____ 6. Don't point that at me

_____ 7. The sun will be setting at 7:47 tonight

_____ 8. We won a trip to Hawaii

_____ 9. May I borrow your car

_____ 10. Take off your shoes and stay awhile

Sentences

You are a doctor specializing in sentences. Today you are working in the emergency room. These sentences need your help immediately. Rewrite each sentence or sentences on the line below it so it will feel better. Remember to capitalize, punctuate, and write complete sentences.

1. my mother and i will be driving a hundred miles today its my grandmas birthday

   _____

2. i have a new puppy his name is lollipop

   _____

3. i said what are you doing

   _____

4. watch out john

   _____

5. have you seen my little brother i think hes lost

   _____

6. i fell into the pool my shoes are wet

   _____

7. we saw mrs hunter at palm elementary school on thursday

   _____

8. my friend lives in northridge california shes really funny

   _____

9. do you like liver

   _____

10. Will you please hold my snake he's hungry

   _____

Writing Sample for Using the Punctuation Tool

Directions: Find punctuation errors. Show the correct punctuation using proofreader's marks.

The two boys went around to the side of the house The cool musty odor of the basement greeted Jonathan as he opened the door. He went down the narrow steps slowly allowing his eyes time to adjust to the darkness. Jonathon rounded the post at the bottom of the stairs and glanced at the shelves. He couldn't decide whether or not to search them thoroughly. Deciding not to, he turned around to survey the rest of the basement and almost bumped into David.

"It's too dark to look very well down here," Jonathon said. I'll never find a key in this mess. If I did, it probably would be rusted and corroded and wouldn't work. He sighed and went up the stairs as slowly as he had gone down.

"Maybe the shop would be a good place to look" David suggested as they stepped around the corner into the backyard. The door to the shop was open, as usual, and Jonathon walked in. Now this, this was a fascinating place, even if it was messy.

"I've got to get serious about finding this key before dinner." Jonathon said "After dinner, I want to play ball with the guys." Jonathon looked around as David stopped to fool with some tools on the workbench. Jonathon didn't see any keys on the workbench. He walked over to look at the pegboard, and sure enough, a key was hanging there Jonathon looked at the key for a minute, studying it.

"It doesn't look like it fits the garage door, but I'll try it to be sure before I take it."

Getting to the Root of Prefixes

The dictionary lists prefixes as entries. These parts of words, when added to a root word, change the word's meaning. Use a dictionary to find the meaning of each prefix below. Next, match its meaning to the prefix.

Prefixes	**Meanings**
_____ 1. un-	A. twice *or* two
_____ 2. re-	B. again
_____ 3. pre-	C. not
_____ 4. mis-	D. bad, wrongly, *or* badly
_____ 5. in-, im-	E. three
_____ 6. bi-	F. before
_____ 7. tri-	G. not *or* a lack of

Now, add the prefixes to a root word below to create a new word. Choose from the root words in the box. Use each root word only once. Check your words in a dictionary.

cycle	annual	produce	caution
tangle	lead	complete	

Prefix	**Root Word**		**New Word**
8. un +	_____	=	_____
9. re +	_____	=	_____
10. pre +	_____	=	_____
11. mis +	_____	=	_____
12. in +	_____	=	_____
13. bi +	_____	=	_____
14. tri +	_____	=	_____

The Prefixes *in-* and *il-*

The prefixes *in-* and *il-* mean "not." The prefix *il-* is added to base words that begin with the letter *l*. The prefix *in-* is added to most other words.

> Examples: *incapable* means "not capable"
>
> *illegible* means "not legible" (not able to be read)

Part I: Write the meaning for each word.

Example: inseparable ____not able to be separated____

1. incorrect _____

2. illogical _____

3. informal _____

4. independent _____

5. invisible _____

6. illegal _____

7. insane _____

8. inaccurate _____

9. incomplete _____

10. ineffective _____

An *antonym* is a word that means the opposite of another. *Sincere* and *insincere* are antonyms.

Part II: Add the prefix *in-* or *il-* to change each word to its antonym.

Example: ability ____inability____

1. secure _____

2. action _____

3. legal _____

4. expensive _____

5. logical _____

6. frequent _____

7. legible _____

8. direct _____

9. justice _____

10. literate (able to read/write) _____

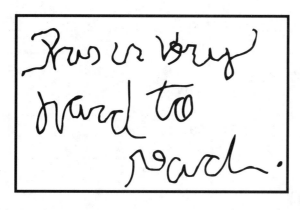

illegible

illegible

illegible

illegible

The Prefix *mis-*

The prefix *mis-* means "wrong."

Thinking of the word *mistake* will help you to remember the meaning.

   Example: misuse means "wrong use"

Part I: Add the prefix *mis* to the base word to form a new word.

   Example: pronounce   <u>mispronounce</u>

1. print _____	7. fire _____
2. fit _____	8. leading _____
3. spoke _____	9. match _____
4. judge _____	10. informed _____
5. spell _____	11. treat _____
6. placed _____	12. fortune _____

Part II: Write a word from the box below that means the opposite of the word or phrase given.

misfortune	mistake	mismanaged	misbehavior
mismatched	mislabel	mislead	misspelled
misjudge	misprint	misquote	~~misunderstood~~

Word	Opposite	Word	Opposite
1. understood	<u>misunderstood</u>	7. label correctly	_____
2. matched	_____	8. quote exactly	_____
3. good behavior	_____	9. print correctly	_____
4. good fortune	_____	10. correct	_____
5. spelled right	_____	11. lead correctly	_____
6. well managed	_____	12. judge correctly	_____

More Practice with the Prefix *over-*

The prefix *over-* means "over (across or above)" or "too much."

overboard	overgrown	overdue	overflowed	overwhelmed	overlap
overpass	overcooked	overweight	overseas	overlooked	overslept

Part I: Choose the word from the box above that best completes each sentence and write it on the line. Each word is used once.

1. The little child felt _____ by the loud noises.

2. When she forgot to shut off the faucet, the sink _____.

3. Jacob _____, which made him late getting to school.

4. The doctor put the _____ man on a diet.

5. Be sure to _____ the edges and press them down with glue.

6. The highway _____ bridge iced up before the road did.

7. My cousin, who is in the Navy, is serving _____ for two years.

8. It is dangerous to fall _____ on a ship.

9. The castle stood on a cliff that _____ the sea.

10. The thicket was so _____ that we couldn't move through it.

11. The _____ meat was too dry.

12. Bryan returned the three _____ DVDs to the library.

Part II: Pick two words from the box above. Use each in a sentence.

Example: If you eat a lot of candy, you may become overweight.

1. _____

   _____

2. _____

   _____

The Suffix *-ing* for Nouns

The suffix *-ing* can mean "the material used to." This suffix comes at the end of nouns (things).

Examples: *icing* is the material used to ice a cake or cookie

plumbing is the material (pipes) used in a water or sewer system

Part I: Write the meaning of each noun.

Example: salad dressing ___material used to "dress" a salad___

1. carpeting _____
2. lighting _____
3. roofing _____
4. stuffing _____
5. clothing _____
6. bedding _____

7. tiling _____
8. leggings _____
9. siding _____
10. styling gel _____
11. flooring _____
12. frosting _____

Part II: Sort the 12 words above into one of three categories. Write the words in the correct place.

Used in a House

Something You Eat

salad dressing

Used on a Body

Adding-*ing* to Verbs

Here are a few rules to follow adding *ing* to a verb:
- The letters *ing* are added to a verb (action word).
- If the word ends with an *e*, drop the *e* and add <u>*ing*</u>.
- If the final letters in the word are a short vowel followed by a single consonant, double the consonant and add *ing*.
- A one-syllable word ending in *ie* will change to *y* before adding the *ing*

	Base + Ending	In Context
burning	burn + ing	The barn was already **burning** when we got there.
breaking	break + ing	The men were **breaking** the rules.
feeling	feel + ing	I've been **feeling** ill today.
giving	give + ing	What are you **giving** him for his birthday?
exciting	excite + ing	We had an **exciting** time at the birthday party.
shining	shine + ing	Yesterday the sun was **shining**.
diving	dive + ing	A girl was **diving** into the deep water.
amazing	amaze + ing	The team did some **amazing** magic tricks for us.
admitting	admit + ing	I'm **admitting** that I did the wrong thing.
winning	win + ing	You must be on a **winning** streak.
grabbing	grab + ing	The baby started **grabbing** his sister's toys.
begging	beg + ing	My kids have been **begging** to go to an amusement park.
tying	tie + ing	The woman started **tying** a rope around her waist.
dying	die + ing	The flowers were all **dying** due to the lack of rain.
lying	lie + ing	There's no sense in **lying** about it.

Copy the spelling words in the order they appear above. Number them in order from A–Z. You may need to look as far as the third letter. Then write the words in A–Z order.

Word Number	Number	A-Z Order
1.		
2.		
3.		
4.		
5.		
6.		
7.		
8.		
9.		
10.		
11.		
12.		
13.		
14.		
15.		

The Suffix -ous

The suffix *-ous* means "full of."

Words ending with the suffix *-ous* are adjectives (words that describe nouns).

Examples: *courteous* means "full of courtesy"

disastrous means "full of disaster"

Part I: For each definition, write an adjective ending with the suffix *-ous*.

Example: full of numbers*   _____numerous_____

1. full of marvel _____

2. full of continue* _____

3. full of danger _____

4. full of courage _____

5. full of miracle* _____

6. full of poison _____

7. full of humor _____

8. full of glamor _____

9. full of fame* _____

10. full of hazard _____

* The base word spelling changes when you add the *-ous*.

A *synonym* is a word that means the same as another. *Dangerous* and *hazardous* are synonyms.

horrendous	enormous	joyous	dangerous	poisonous	courteous
numerous	~~gorgeous~~	humorous	marvelous	courageous	famous

Part II: Write the word from the box above that is the synonym of the word(s) given.

Word	Synonym	Word	Synonym
1. beautiful	gorgeous	7. wonderful	_____
2. well-known	_____	8. joyful	_____
3. many	_____	9. gigantic	_____
4. harmful	_____	10. brave	_____
5. polite	_____	11. awful; terrible	_____
6. toxic; deadly	_____	12. funny	_____

28

The Suffix -*tion*

The suffix -*tion* means "state or quality of." It is pronounced "shun." Adding the suffix -*tion* usually changes a word into a noun (thing).

> *Examples:* **fascination** means "state of being fascinated"
>
> **option** means "having the quality of opting" (choosing)

Part I: Change these words into nouns by adding -*tion* as a suffix. Check the spelling of the starred words in the dictionary before writing them on the lines.

Example: move* _____motion_____

1. attend* _____
2. invent _____
3. pollute* _____
4. direct _____
5. revolve* _____
6. reflect _____
7. explain* _____
8. complete* _____
9. determine* _____
10. protect _____
11. react _____
12. quote* _____
13. repeat* _____
14. prevent _____
15. combine* _____
16. exclaim* _____

* The spelling of a base word that ends in a letter other than *t* always changes when the suffix -*tion* is added.

Part II: Look at the changes you made to the starred words above. Write the words on the correct stars below.

| **Drop Final Letter,** | **Drop Final Letter,** | **Change Base Word,** |
| Add –*tion* | Add Vowel and -*tion* | Add -*tion* |

The Suffix *-sion*

The suffix *-sion* means "state or quality of." It is pronounced "shun." When *-sion* is added to a verb (action word), it changes the word to a noun.

Examples: **collision** is what occurs when things collide (come into contact with each other)

decision is the result of a person deciding (making a choice)

Part I: Add *-sion* to each of the following verbs to form a noun. Check the spelling of the starred words in the dictionary before writing them on the lines.

Example: expand* _____expansion_____

1. confess _____
2. include* _____
3. televise* _____
4. discuss _____
5. admit* _____

6. comprehend* _____
7. profess _____
8. extend* _____
9. invade* _____
10. conclude* _____

* The spelling of a verb that ends in a letter other than *s* always changes when the suffix *-sion* is added.

Part II: Name the verb that is the basis for each of the following nouns. If you get stumped, you may use a dictionary.

Example: erosion _____erode_____

1. decision _____
2. division _____
3. exclusion _____
4. conclusion _____
5. explosion _____

6. revision _____
7. invasion _____
8. tension _____
9. confusion _____
10. permission _____

Dividing Words by Syllables

Dividing words can be a tricky business, but if you know the rule outlined below, it will become a snap. Read the rule carefully and apply your knowledge to the words below.

> ## Rule
> When a word has a double consonant, the word is divided between the two consonants.
>
> **Example:** bub´-ble

Divide each word below into syllables, and place a stressed syllable mark (´) on the syllable you think is stressed. Use a dictionary to check your answers.

1. borrow _____

2. attic _____

3. banner _____

4. blizzard _____

5. effect _____

6. flutter _____

7. hobby _____

8. lettuce _____

9. mitten _____

10. stallion _____

11. soccer _____

12. pattern _____

13. stubborn _____

14. puzzle _____

15. ladder _____

16. follow _____

17. butter _____

Synonyms Are Similar

Synonyms are words that mean the same, or about the same, as another word. To find a synonym we use the *thesaurus*. Using synonyms in your writing helps keep writing fresh and helps us to avoid overusing words. Here is an example of a sentence that could use a few synonyms: *The good boy ate a very good lunch and said, "That was good."*

Use your thesaurus to find a synonym for each of the following words.

1. ache _____

2. argue _____

3. bulge _____

4. check _____

5. earnest _____

6. flutter _____

7. hesitate _____

8. jealous _____

9. locate _____

10. murmur _____

11. object _____

12. perform _____

13. prance _____

14. scamper _____

15. tilt _____

Now pick two of the synonyms from above and use them in a sentence. _____

_____

_____

Pick two more and use them in another sentence. _____

_____

_____

32

Antonyms: Opposites Attract

Antonyms are words that mean the opposite of each other. For example: *good* and *bad*, *quiet* and *noisy*.

Look at the words in column 1. Find the antonym for each word in column 2. Write the letter of the antonym in column 2 next to its match in column 1. The first one has been done for you.

Column 1	Column 2
_F_ 1. accept	A. lose
_____ 2. bury	B. begin
_____ 3. crooked	C. modesty
_____ 4. disgust	D. approval
_____ 5. familiar	E. strange
_____ 6. gloomy	F. refuse
_____ 7. hungry	G. straight
_____ 8. locate	H. bright
_____ 9. mysterious	I. unearth
_____ 10. nonsense	J. untrustworthy
_____ 11. obey	K. obvious
_____ 12. pride	L. full
_____ 13. quit	M. wisdom
_____ 14. responsible	N. fat
_____ 15. slender	O. ignore

Rules for Plurals

Make a singular noun plural by adding *s*.

A noun is a person, place, or thing. When a noun is just one person, place, or thing, we say it is *singular*. For example, in the sentence "The girl walked away," the noun *girl* is singular. When the noun is talking about more than one person, place, or thing, we say the noun is *plural*. In the sentence "The girls walked away," the noun *girls* is plural. By adding *s* to the noun, we show we are speaking about more than one girl.

Directions: Add *s* to the following words to show the plural form of the noun.

Singular	Plural
1. car	_____
2. desk	_____
3. house	_____
4. tree	_____
5. boy	_____

We can't just add an *s* to every noun to make it plural, though. For nouns ending in *ch*, *s*, *sh*, *ss*, *x*, or *z*, we must add *es* to form the plural.

Add *es* to the following nouns to change them from singular to plural.

Singular	Plural
6. box	_____
7. church	_____
8. dish	_____
9. dress	_____
10. waltz	_____
11. sketch	_____
12. lens	_____
13. tax	_____
14. business	_____
15. glass	_____

Language Arts

Plurals

Here are a few rules about plurals:
- Plurals show more than one.
- Usually you do this by adding *s* to the end of the word.
- However, if the word ends in *s, o, x, z, ch* or *sh*, you must add *es*.

Word	Base + Ending	In Context
friends	friend + s	He has six **friends** in that class.
answers	answer + s	She knew all the **answers** to the test questions.
sentences	sentence + s	The teacher said to write at least six **sentences**.
weddings	wedding + s	I have three **weddings** to attend this month.
minutes	minute + s	After about ten **minutes**, the taxi arrived.
buses	bus + es	Four **buses** passed me before one stopped.
glasses	glass + es	I filled three **glasses** with milk.
addresses	address + es	The book contains people's names and **addresses**.
potatoes	potato + es	Mom bought a five-pound sack of **potatoes**.
mosquitoes	mosquito + es	We had to come inside because **mosquitoes** were biting us.
boxes	box + es	The **boxes** spilled out from beneath the Christmas tree.
branches	branch + es	The tree's **branches** broke under the weight of the ice.
sandwiches	sandwich + es	Please fix us some peanut butter **sandwiches**.
dishes	dish + es	I'll put these **dishes** on the table.
bushes	bush + es	Let's plant some **bushes** in that corner of the yard.

Write each spelling word on the correct line in column two. Then, in column three, show which letters need to be added to make the word plural and why.

Singular	Plural	Reason Plural Appears this Way
ex. table	tables	add *s* to show more than one
ex. tomato	tomatoes	add *es* to words ending with *o*
1. bush		
2. friend		
3. potato		
4. dish		
5. minute		
6. sentence		
7. sandwich		
8. address		
9. mosquito		
10. branch		
11. wedding		
12. box		
13. answer		
14. bus		
15. glass		

Identifying and Spelling Homophones

A homophone is a word that sounds the same as another word but has a different meaning and different spelling.

Use a word from the box to complete each sentence.

poor	tail	pour	tale
wood	hear	would	here

1. Our teacher told us a _____ about a dinosaur.

2. Did you _____ the roar of the lions at the zoo?

3. Ricardo and Luke cut some _____ to make a campfire.

4. I asked Lucille to _____ the water in the bottle.

5. Rosa's dog spun around and tried to bite its own _____.

6. I asked Ms. Lucky to leave the books right _____.

7. Luke was too _____ to buy even a hamburger for lunch.

8. Ricky said he _____ come if he had his parents' permission.

Underline the correct words in the parentheses.

9. Lucy told Rosa it is rude to (**stair, stare**) at people.

10. They watched the old ship being (**towed, toad**) out to sea to be sunk.

11. Did you (**meet, meat**) our new teacher, Ricardo?

12. Luke brushed his favorite horse's (**main, mane**).

13. Our family's new automobile is made of a special kind of (**steal, steel**).

14. Unfortunately, Lucille's mother was too (**weak, week**) to leave the hospital.

15. Our parents tell us we should not (**medal, meddle**) in other people's business.

16. Luke (**rode, road**) up on his favorite horse, Bronco.

17. It is almost time for our daily (**male, mail**) delivery.

18. I used stone-ground (**flower, flour**) to make the biscuits.

Context Clues Practice

Directions: The underlined words in the following sentences are French words. Use the context clues to figure out the meaning of each word. Write the meaning in the blank.

1. That pen is broken. Throw it in the corbeille.

   Corbeille means _____.

2. The dentist told me I had a cavity. He tells me I must brosser my teeth at least twice a day.

   Brosser means _____.

3. Write this down because I do not want you to oublier it.

   Oublier means _____.

4. My grandma lives on a farm and has lots of farm animals. When I spend the night with her I am always awakened by the coq early in the morning.

   Coq means _____.

5. She cleaned up her room so lentement that I thought it would take her all day to get the job done.

   Lentement means _____.

More Context Clues Practice

Directions: The **boldface underlined** words in the following sentences are unusual words. Use the context clues to figure out the meaning of each word. Write a sentence to explain what you think each underlined word means.

1. Have you ever been to a farm where they have **kine**? The farm I went to was a milking farm so they didn't use the **kine** for meat.

   _____

   _____

2. My coach is so **fastidious**. It seems like no matter how hard we work she's not pleased.

   _____

   _____

3. I think I would have enjoyed the card game much more if my big sister had not been such a **kibitzer**. I got very tired of her hanging over my shoulder to give me tips.

   _____

   _____

4. After Attila's team won the championship, they **jubilated** together. The coach bought the team ice cream and they congratulated each other all evening.

   _____

   _____

What Is the Cause?
What Is the Effect?

Directions: Complete the chart below. The left side of the chart is for causes, and the right side of the chart is for effects. Make sure that your answers make sense.

Cause	Effect
1. I tripped on the steps at school.	1. _____ _____ _____
2. _____ _____ _____	2. We were soaking wet!
3. I scored the winning goal in our soccer game.	3. _____ _____ _____
4. _____ _____ _____	4. My mom is very happy today
5. I completed my homework.	5. _____ _____ _____

Cause and Effect

Directions: Read "The Runner" carefully and then complete the chart on page 41.

The Runner

When Bradley saw his cousin compete in the State Racing Championships, he began to dream that he would one day compete in the State Racing Championships. Since his dream was so strong, Bradley began to organize races in his neighborhood on the weekends with other neighborhood kids. To prepare for these neighborhood races, Bradley would run every day after school. Sometimes he even borrowed his grandma's stopwatch and timed himself.

When Bradley began middle school, he signed up to be on the track team. Bradley had to run and practice very hard to stay on the track team, but he wanted to compete in the State Racing Championship so much that he kept working hard. Three years later Bradley successfully tried out for the high school track team. Bradley realized that he not only had to work hard at running, but he also had to work hard at his schoolwork. All members of the track team had to keep their grades up so that they could continue to participate.

Bradley kept his grades up and proved that he was a committed student and track team member. When he was a senior in high school he had the opportunity to compete in the Regional Racing Championships . . . and he won! One month later he was fulfilling his dream by competing in the State Racing Championships.

On the day of the State Racing Championships, Bradley was very nervous. He knew he would be competing against some of the best runners in the state, but he decided that he needed to focus on his own running and not worry about the other runners. All of Bradley's years of hard work finally paid off when he brought home the State Racing Championships second-place trophy.

40

The Runner

Directions: Carefully read "The Runner" and complete the chart below. Write one cause-and-effect event in each box in the order they occurred. You will not need to use every cause-and-effect event in the story.

Cause	
Effect	

Cause	
Effect	

Cause	
Effect	

Cause	
Effect	

Cause	
Effect	

Prediction

Directions: Carefully read "Belize?" and then complete the prediction chart on page 43 with your predictions about what Julia's next letter will contain. Write your predictions on the left side of the chart. On the right side of the chart, write what caused you to think of the predictions.

Belize?

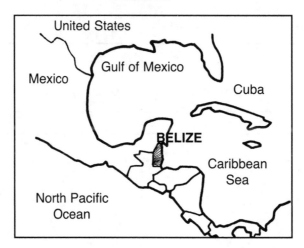

September 22, 2003

Dear Friend,

Greetings! My name is Julia, and I am fifteen years old. Two years ago I went to Belize to visit friends with my parents. I had a blast and learned a lot! Do you know where Belize is? Have you ever heard of plantain? Do you know what a tapir is? Have you ever tasted corn ice cream? I am guessing that your answer was "no" to most of those questions, and that is why I am writing this letter to you. Belize has a lot of great things that not too many kids know about. I hope that my letters will help you learn more about this great country!

First of all, I should tell you where in the world Belize is. Belize is a country in Central America. Mexico and Guatemala are Belize's neighbors. I will try and tell you more about them later. The capital city of Belize is Belmopan, located in the center of the country. We spent most of our time in the large city of Belize City and the small town of San Ignacio.

Belize has many beautiful sights, but one of my favorite things about Belize is the people! I was able to visit several schools and churches in Belize and hang out with our old and new friends. So what do kids do for fun in Belize? Some kids probably do a lot of the same things that you do. Our friends' kids go to school on the weekdays, go to church on the weekend, help their parents with work at home, play ball with their friends, and buy sweets at the store.

There are many more things that I want to tell you about Belize and my experiences, but that will have to be kept for the next letter.

So long,

Julia

Prediction

Belize? *(cont.)*

Predictions About What Julia Will Write in Her Second Letter	Reasons Why I Made the Predictions
1.	1.
2.	2.
3.	3.
4.	4.
5.	5.

Inference

Directions: Read "Lena" and then record facts from the story that give you clues as to what Lena's job is. Finally, make an inference about what Lena's job is.

Lena

When Lena entered her office, she put down her briefcase and anxiously listened to her answering machine messages. She jotted down the phone numbers of the three people who called, grabbed her notebook and pen, and dialed the first number on her list. "Wow! Really? They found it in the backyard? Now, that's news!" she said. Lena asked the caller a series of questions and feverishly took notes as the person answered the questions. After making all of her calls, Lena began typing up the information she had gained. "This'll be great for the front page!" she exclaimed.

Clues (*facts from the story*)

_____

_____

_____

_____

_____

_____

Inference (*conclusion about what Lena's job is*)

_____

_____

_____

_____

_____

_____

_____

Inference

Directions: The following story gives you many clues about what Daryl and his family are planning to do. Read the story carefully and then answer the questions that follow it.

Changes

Daryl couldn't believe the day was finally here! His mother woke him up early and rushed him to breakfast. "Make sure you wash your own bowl and put it back, Daryl," his mother said, "I don't want dirty dishes left behind." Daryl reached into a box filled with newspaper-wrapped dishes and pulled out a bowl for his breakfast.

As Daryl finished washing his dish, his best friend, Larry, came to the back door. "Hey, Daryl! I thought I'd better bring this sweatshirt over to you," he explained. "You left it at my house awhile back. It might be awhile before I see you again."

"Thanks," Daryl replied with a smile. "I wondered what happened to that."

"Yeah, and you're probably going to really need it now," Larry stated. "No more beach clothes for you!"

"Yeah," said Daryl, "But I'm ready for a change."

---

1. What can you infer from this story? What are Daryl and his family getting ready to do? (Be as specific as you can.)

_____

_____

_____

2. What clues helped you to make this inference? List at least three specific clues from the story.

_____

_____

_____

Main Idea

Directions: Read the following paragraph. Then identify the main idea and write two supporting details. Write them in the graphic organizer below.

Tiger

Tiger was the funniest cat we have ever had. He was the first cat to start drinking from our fish aquarium. I would laugh so hard every time I saw Tiger perched up on the fish aquarium, lapping up water from the water filter system! He never bothered the fish; he just loved to drink their water! Another funny thing that Tiger did was drink from the dog's bath water. Whenever we would be giving the dog a bath, Tiger would waltz over and start lapping up water from the tub. I don't think the dog appreciated that, but we sure thought it was funny! Tiger was definitely a very funny cat.

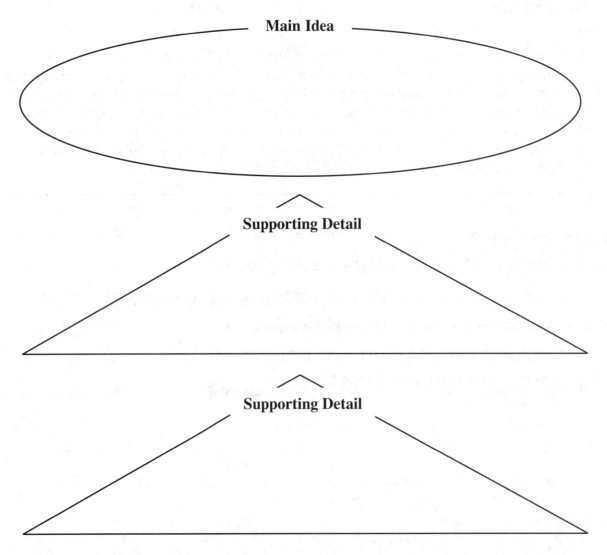

Main Idea

Supporting Detail

Supporting Detail

Identifying the Main Idea

The Grand Canyon in Arizona is one of the natural wonders of the world. The Canyon's rim towers over the Colorado River far below. This river has snaked through the Canyon for millions of years. During this time it has carved its way through many layers of rock. This left rock layers exposed. The different colors show the various types of rocks in each layer. The part closest to the river is black. The layer above it is a brilliant red. The next layer looks brown or light purple. It depends on how the sunlight hits it. The Grand Canyon has other layers, too. Its top layer is dull gray limestone.

What is the main idea?

Choose from the answers below and fill the bubble by your choice.

ⓐ The Grand Canyon in Arizona is one of the natural wonders of the world.

ⓑ The Grand Canyon has many different rock layers.

ⓒ The top layer of the Grand Canyon is dull gray limestone.

ⓓ The Colorado River carved the Grand Canyon.

Determining the Main Idea

The main idea is not always stated. One way to figure out an unstated main idea is to make a "movie in your mind."

It was a warm night for the end of October, so the trick-or-treaters didn't have to wear jackets over their outfits. Dressed in her angel costume, Sofia skipped from door to door. She wanted to go to each house on the street.

One house near the end of the block had its front door standing open with the screen door shut. Light spilled from within. Sofia rang the bell and waited on the steps. A large black dog raced up to the screen door, barking loudly. A young woman appeared and pushed the dog away. She opened the door just far enough to offer a basketful of candy to Sofia. As Sofia reached into the basket, she was knocked flat on the ground. The dog stood on all fours over her, barking. Sofia screamed.

What is the main idea?

Choose from the answers below and fill the bubble by your choice.

ⓐ While out trick-or-treating, Sofia is terrified when a dog leaps on top of her.

ⓑ Sofia is greedy because she wants to get candy from every house on her street.

ⓒ Sofia gets candy at a house with a dog.

ⓓ Sofia enjoys wearing her angel costume on Halloween.

Top Five Children's Books

Read the passage below and answer the questions.

Recently thousands of students aged 7 to 15 voted. They chose the top five kids' books. Number one is a series. It's the Harry Potter books by J. K. Rowling. Second place is the Goosebumps series by R. L. Stine. Dr. Seuss wrote the third and fourth place titles. *Green Eggs and Ham* and *The Cat in the Hat* are favorites for new readers. Marc Brown writes the fifth place winner, the Arthur series.

What does this mean? Kids love the adventure and fantasy in *Harry Potter*. They like to read scary stuff, too, as long as it isn't too frightening. That's why 300 million copies of the Goosebumps series have been sold. Dr. Seuss showed humor does well with young kids. The Arthur series works because every kid can relate to one of the characters.

1. You can infer that the children's series that has now sold the most copies is
   a. the Harry Potter series.
   b. the Goosebumps series.
   c. the Arthur series.

2. The authors of the top five kids' books are probably
   a. poor.
   b. rich.
   c. uneducated.

3. A type of fiction that most students didn't vote for is
   a. fantasy.
   b. science fiction.
   c. humor.

4. The third most popular children's book title is
   a. *Arthur*.
   b. *The Cat in the Hat*.
   c. *Green Eggs and Ham*.

Chocolate Woes

Read the passage below and answer the questions.

The price of chocolate is rising. Why? There's less chocolate. That makes it worth more money. So why don't the candy companies just make more chocolate? Fewer beans are coming from Brazil, in South America. A disease hurt their cacao trees. Many of the trees have died.

Cacao trees grow cacao beans. Chocolate comes from these beans. There are lots of different kinds of cacao beans. Each candy company has its own recipe for chocolate. They must blend different beans together to get their kind of chocolate.

Brazil's farmers are working to save their trees. They spray them with chemicals. They've made progress. Even so, in 2000 the bean harvest was the worst in 30 years. If this problem isn't solved, it may someday cost $5 for a candy bar!

1. Cacao trees grow in
   a. North America.
   b. Central America.
   c. South America.

2. Which statement is false?
   a. Cacao farmers have saved all their trees.
   b. Each chocolate maker uses its own recipe.
   c. Chocolate is made with cacao beans.

3. Of the following choices, which happened first?
   a. There were fewer cacao beans.
   b. The price of chocolate rose.
   c. Cacao trees got a disease.

4. Chocolate is frequently given as a gift on
   a. Valentine's Day.
   b. the Fourth of July.
   c. Labor Day weekend.

Let's Stop Bullies

Read the passage below and answer the questions.

Bullies like to push other kids around and call them names. No one wants to be a bully's target.   Yet every year five million kids are victims. There are girl bullies as well as boy bullies. About 160,000 kids skip school daily just to avoid them.

What should you do if a bully bothers you? Ignore the bully. Turn and walk away. Don't act afraid and don't cry. That will just encourage the bully. Immediately tell an adult. Adults will know what to do about the bully.

Schools want to stop bullying. Some have *implemented* programs to show why bullying is wrong. The lessons teach students to never hit or say mean things. It has worked with some bullies. When they begin feeling bad about hurting others, they stop their cruel behavior.

1. Which is a behavior a bully might do?
    a. accidentally spill milk on a kid at lunch
    b. deliberately trip a kid carrying a lunch tray
    c. laugh when someone tells a joke

2. What's the best thing to do if a bully is being mean to another kid?
    a. Fight with the bully.
    b. Tell an adult immediately.
    c. Turn and walk away without doing anything.

3. Some schools started programs to stop bullying because they want students to
    a. understand the basics of a democracy.
    b. learn how to use karate to defend themselves.
    c. attend school instead of staying home due to bullies.

4. The word *implemented* means
    a. talked about.
    b. thrown away.
    c. put into practice.

Helmets Are Cool

Read the passage below and answer the questions.

If you think you don't need to wear a helmet, you're wrong. In fact, anyone who doesn't wear a helmet whenever on wheels is foolish. Riding a bike, scooter, skateboard, or skates without a helmet is *hazardous*. Why? Riders can get serious head injuries.

How do helmets help? They protect your brain. Each year more than 400,000 kids end up in the hospital with head injuries that could have been avoided. Even worse, 500 die just because they failed to put on helmets. They thought they didn't need them.

If worn correctly, a helmet reduces your chance of head injury in an accident by 85 percent. Worn correctly means that the helmet fits well and is buckled. Always wear a helmet! It could save your life.

1. Why is it so important to protect your head?
   a. Your brain controls all of your body's parts.
   b. You'd look ugly with a bump on your head.
   c. If you fell a certain way, you'd lose all your hair and become bald.

2. An unbuckled helmet
   a. works as well as a buckled helmet.
   b. is the best way to wear a helmet.
   c. will probably fly off your head during an accident.

3. How many kids die each year because they didn't wear a helmet?
   a. 85
   b. 500
   c. 400,000

4. A synonym for *hazardous* is
   a. silly.
   b. annoying.
   c. dangerous.

Clown Fish

Read the passage below and answer the questions.

Have you seen the movie *Finding Nemo*? Nemo and his dad are clown fish. In the film Nemo's dad has to avoid dangers in order to rescue Nemo. In the ocean clown fish have found a way to use danger to their advantage.

Clown fish are colored bright orange and white. Predators can easily see them. So they stay safe by living inside the "branches" of the sea anemone. The sea anemone looks like a small bush. But its branches are actually poisonous tentacles. The anemone uses them as defense against enemies. It also uses them to grab and sting food.

The sea anemone stings the clown fish. But it is *unaffected* by the venom. So it hides in the midst of the tentacles. No other fish can reach the clown fish without getting stung itself.

1. When would a clown fish leave the sea anemone's tentacles?
   a. to seek safety
   b. to find food
   c. to chase away predators

2. Which statement is false?
   a. Clown fish must be careful to avoid the sea anemone's sting.
   b. Clown fish are bright orange and white.
   c. Many of the animals that eat clown fish are afraid of sea anemones.

3. The clown fish's reaction to the sea anemone is most like
   a. a person rubbing against poison ivy without getting a rash.
   b. a fish being grabbed by the tentacles of an octopus.
   c. a person allergic to nuts.

4. In this article the word *unaffected* means
   a. killed instantly.
   b. made stronger.
   c. unharmed.

Top Board Games in America

Read the passage below and answer the questions.

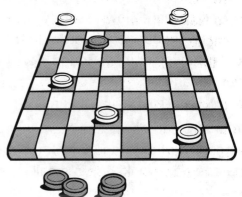

Do you like board games? Many people do. They have been played for thousands of years. There were board games in Ancient Greece and Rome. The oldest known one is about 4,500 years old. Long ago players threw dice and moved pieces around a track in a race to the finish line.

In 1933 the game of Monopoly® was invented in a small U.S. town. Now it's played in 80 countries. It comes in 26 different languages. Over 200 million sets have been sold worldwide.

Monopoly, however, isn't the most popular game in the U.S. Trivial Pursuit® is number one. Second is Cranium®, and Monopoly® takes third place. Other top games include the Game of Life® and Scrabble®. Chess and checkers, two old favorites, have been played for hundreds of years.

1. The most popular board game in America is
   a. Cranium®.
   b. Monopoly®.
   c. Trivial Pursuit®.

2. Based on the facts given, where was Monopoly® created?
   a. Rome
   b. Pennsylvania
   c. Greece

3. Which statement is false?
   a. Board games were played at least 4,000 years ago.
   b. Many board games use dice.
   c. The game of Monopoly® is printed in 80 different languages.

4. Of the following choices, which happened last?
   a. People played Cranium®.
   b. People in Ancient Rome played board games.
   c. People played chess.

Basketball

Read the passage below and answer the questions.

The game of basketball started in December 1891. Dr. James Naismith, a gym teacher, wanted to try a new idea. He emptied two bushel baskets. Then he cut the bottoms out of the baskets. He nailed one basket up on the balcony at each end of the gym. The goal was to get the ball into the other team's basket.

Players started with the ball in the middle of the gym. The rules said they could throw or bat the ball with any part of their body. But there was no dribbling. Dribbling started in 1929.

Professional games were played starting in 1896. Teams toured the country. They earned money based on the ticket sales. In 1949 the National Basketball Association was formed. Today's top players earn millions of dollars each year.

1. Shaquille O'Neal earns $17 million each year as a pro basketball player. How does that compare to the wages earned by the first players who toured the U.S.?
   a. It is much less money.
   b. It is much more money.
   c. It is about the same amount of money.

2. You can conclude that
   a. the National Basketball Association does not have any rules.
   b. the rules for basketball haven't been changed since 1896.
   c. new rules were added for basketball in 1929.

3. What equipment is necessary to play basketball?
   a. an attached hoop and ball
   b. a ball and bat
   c. a racquet and a ball

4. A synonym for *association* is
   a. team.
   b. organization.
   c. sport.

Community Message Board

Read these messages, then answer the questions on page 57.

Choir Practice
7:30 every Wednesday night. 10th Street Baptist Church. Meet in fellowship hall.

Karate Classes
Teacher has a black belt in karate. Two classes weekly, Wed. and Thurs., 6 p.m. Learn to defend yourself and have fun!

Volunteer Firehouse Pancake Supper, Saturday 5 p.m.–7 p.m.

Moving Sale
56 East Grove Street
Selling furniture, toys, clothes, a bike. Washer and dryer, $100.00 for both

Need your lawn mowed?
I will work hard. Call Mike at: 555–8721

Little League Tryouts
Little League tryouts this Saturday afternoon at 1:00. Call Brad at 555–2941 for more information. Bring your own glove.

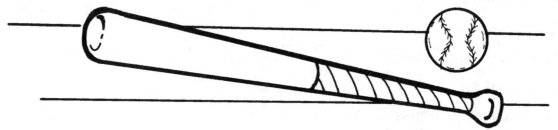

Dog Wash in Marlow Park.
Bring your dog. We'll wash it! $5.00 per dog. Flea dip extra. Call Lisa at 555–0971 for more information.

New Day to Recycle is Wednesday
Recycling pick-up day has been changed. It is now Wednesday. Be sure to put your recycling on the curb before 8:00 a.m.

Community Message Board *(cont.)*

1. When should you put your recycling on the curb?

    a. Wednesday afternoon

    b. After 8:00 a.m. on Wednesday

    c. At 8:00 a.m. on Wednesday

    d. Before 8:00 a.m. on Wednesday

2. The reason the message board is in a store in the middle of town is

    a. the store was paid to put it there.

    b. to make sure everyone sees it.

    c. it is near Marlow Park.

    d. it is near the Baptist Church.

3. Who is the message board for?

    a. Only dog owners

    b. Everybody in the community

    c. Only people who are moving

    d. Everyone in the neighboring town

4. Which of these is a fact found on the message board?

    a. All of the dogs in the community have fleas.

    b. Mike needs his lawn mowed.

    c. Only the Baptist Church has a choir.

    d. The little league does not give players gloves.

5. Which of these does the Community Message Board most resemble?

    a. A story about another town

    b. A public notice about a Town Hall meeting

    c. A true story about the town

    d. A letter mailed to the Baptist Church

Flea Market Find

Bethany loved to go with her mom and dad to the flea market. This Saturday morning was a perfect flea-market day, bright and sunny but not too warm. Mom turned the car onto the crunchy gravel road. A man in an old baseball cap stood in the road. Mom slowed down and gave the man a dollar. He handed her a ticket. Bethany smiled and waved at the man. He waved back.

Mom drove slowly, looking for a place to park. Bethany watched the people walking around the booths. Some booths had bright banners hanging from them. One read: Pillows For Sale, 2 for $20. Another said: All Shoes 50% OFF. A third said: The World's Biggest Waffles. Mom found a parking space and they all got out of the car.

They did the same thing every weekend. First, they went to Bubba's Hot Drinks stand. Mom and Dad bought coffee, and Bethany got hot chocolate. Mom and Bethany shared a blueberry muffin while Dad ate a bagel. After they ate, it was time to shop!

There was always something new at the flea market. Bethany, Mom, and Dad wandered from booth to booth. Mom bought a bunch of dried flowers. Dad looked at all the shiny tools in the tool booth. One man had a booth filled with wind-up toys. Bethany laughed at the wind-up toy dog that barked and jumped.

"Do you see anything you like?" Mom asked. Bethany looked around. One booth had hundreds of sweet-smelling candles. In another booth, an artist had paintings for sale. A gray-haired woman in a purple hat sold old curtains. A man wearing a turban had a booth filled with rugs.

"Not yet, Mom," Bethany said. "I'll keep looking, though."

Sometimes Mom stopped to look at something. Dad wandered off to a booth filled with old boat parts. Bethany tasted a sample of homemade fudge that one vendor was giving away. As she chewed the crumbly fudge, her eye caught a booth she had never seen before. It was filled with old stuff. A pile of crates stood in one corner. Wooden picture frames leaned against each other beside a pile of bed frames. Sitting on top of a pile of quilts was an old rag doll.

Bethany looked closely at the doll. The doll had seen better days. Her brown yarn hair was twisted and matted. Bethany could see that her dress had been pretty once, but now it was dirty and torn. The doll dress was made out of purple fabric with tiny pink flowers, and one of her shoes was missing. As tattered as it was, there was something about the doll that Bethany liked.

Bethany's mom and dad came up behind her. "She looks pretty torn up, honey," Mom said. "Are you sure you want her?"

Bethany studied the doll's face. The doll's black-bead eyes looked calmly back.

"Yes, she needs a good home," Bethany said. "Can I have her?"

"Sure," Mom said. After they paid the man at the booth, Bethany carried the doll carefully back to the car. Bethany held her new doll. Yes, there was no doubt about it; she loved the flea market!

58

Flea Market Find *(cont.)*

1. Mom drove slowly in order to
    a. buy some waffles.
    b. find a place to park.
    c. look at the shiny tools.
    d. pay for the rag doll.

2. One of the banners read
    a. Pillows, 50% OFF
    b. All Shoes, 50% OFF
    c. World's Biggest Pillows
    d. Bagels, 2 For $1

3. The story could also be called
    a. "Mom's Day at the Flea Market"
    b. "Bethany's Special Doll"
    c. "Dad Likes Tools"
    d. "Saturday Shopping Spree"

4. How did Bethany probably feel at the end of the story?
    a. Angry
    b. Happy
    c. Upset
    d. Sad

5. According to the story, Bethany is the kind of girl who
    a. likes to sit on top of a pile of quilts.
    b. eats a lot of waffles.
    c. enjoys seeing and finding all sorts of things.
    d. does not like to go to the flea market with her parents.

Mona Wants A Dog

Ever since her friend Claire got a dog last year, Mona had wanted a dog. Mona got to play with Claire's dog every time she went over to Claire's house, which made her want one even more. Mona couldn't stop thinking about it. She checked out books from the library about dogs. She learned what to feed them and when to feed them. She knew the right kinds of toys to give puppies. She knew what kinds of toys older dogs like.

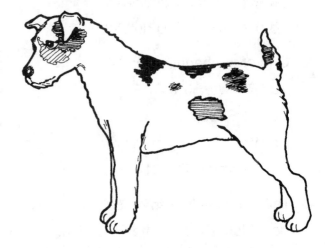

Whenever she had time after school, Mona would go to the computer lab. She liked to look at her favorite website, "Dog Lover's Heaven." It had lists of dogs that were available in her area. She could also find out about every kind of dog in the world. Sometimes, Mona would read about dogs just because their names sounded interesting, like Lhasa apso or Pug. But Mona knew she wanted a Jack Russell terrier because Jack Russells are small and very smart dogs.

One day after school, Mona visited the "Dog Lover's Heaven" website to see what dogs could be adopted. Then she saw it—her dog! It was a male Jack Russell terrier, white with brown spots. He was only a few weeks old. Mona was delighted when she saw the picture of the tiny puppy. She decided that she couldn't wait any longer. When she got home, she found her mother, who was working in the yard. "Can I get a dog, Mom?" she asked.

"We've talked about this, Mona," Mom said. "We have to be sure you can take care of it. It's a lot of work to own a dog."

"But I've done lots of research, Mom," Mona explained.

"I know, but I need to be sure. A dog has to be fed and have lots of water. You have to take it for walks so it can get exercise. Are you ready to do that every day after school, even if you're tired or it's raining?" Mom asked.

"Yes, Mom. I know it's important to you that I take care of it all by myself," Mona said.

"If you get a puppy, it may not be housebroken. Are you going to clean up after it?" Mom asked.

Mona thought for a moment. She knew she wasn't going to like every single thing about owning a dog. Still, a little extra work was a small price to pay for having a great dog. "Yes, Mom," she said. "I will."

"All right, I believe you. Remember what I said about saving your money to pay for the things the dog will need?"

"Yes, Mom," Mona said. "I saved enough already for the Humane Society's adoption fee and for the first visit to the vet. I have been thinking about this for a long time."

"Great!" Mom said. "Then we'll go this weekend. Do you know what kind of dog you want?"

"I sure do," Mona said with a smile. "And I can't wait to meet him!"

Mona Wants a Dog *(cont.)*

1. Mona wanted a dog because

    a. her friend Claire got a dog last year.

    b. she saw a cute commercial on TV.

    c. she walks by a pet store every day.

    d. her teacher talks about her dog.

2. What type of dog does Mona want?

    a. Boston terrier

    b. Lhasa apso

    c. Pug

    d. Jack Russell terrier

3. What does Mona mean when she says "a little extra work was a small price to pay for having a great dog"?

    a. Mona will get a job to help pay for the puppy.

    b. Mona's mom will have to work more hours to afford a puppy.

    c. The dog was on sale, and Mona could work at the pet store.

    d. Mona will not mind cleaning up after a dog.

4. What does Mona's mother mean when she says, "It's a lot of work to own a dog"?

    a. Mona needs to do more research before she is ready to own a dog.

    b. Dogs work hard to be good pets for people.

    c. Dogs have to be fed and exercised every day and cleaned up after.

    d. Mona will need more rest if she gets a dog.

5. How did Mona learn so much about dogs?

    a. Listening to her teacher at school

    b. Visiting an Internet website

    c. Writing to the Humane Society

    d. Watching a videotape about dogs

Starting a Business

Stephanie and Becky had lived next door to each other for as long as they could remember. When they turned seven, both girls received puppies for their birthdays. They worked very hard training the puppies. When the girls were nine, they had two very well trained dogs.

"I think that we did a good job training our dogs," Becky said one day. "What do you think about the idea of starting a dog training business?"

Stephanie's ears perked up. "I think that's a great idea!" she exclaimed. "Let's get started right away."

The girls began their new business by making some flyers on Becky's computer. Then, they hopped on their bikes and pedaled through the neighborhood, passing out the flyers. Many of Stephanie and Becky's neighbors had seen the girls training their own dogs and were very impressed. It wasn't long before the phone was ringing off the hook and the girls had a lot of customers.

During the next few weeks, Becky and Stephanie trained almost every dog in the neighborhood. They worked just as hard as they had with their own dogs. Soon the neighborhood dogs were sitting, fetching, and walking on leashes. The girls received a lot of praise from their customers and were thrilled with their own success.

"Let's send notes thanking everyone for their business," suggested Stephanie. "That way we're sure to get more customers next summer!"

"Now that's what I call a great idea!" Becky laughed.

62

Starting a Business *(cont.)*

1. How does the author present Stephanie and Becky?

   a. As computer experts

   b. As excited and hard-working

   c. As people with a lot of pets

   d. As difficult to get along with

2. How did the girls' customers probably feel after Stephanie and Becky trained the customers' dogs?

   a. Angry

   b. Disappointed

   c. Upset

   d. Glad

3. Which word best describes Stephanie and Becky as they started their new business?

   a. Eager

   b. Careful

   c. Lazy

   d. Hasty

4. What is the main idea of this passage?

   a. Stephanie and Becky both received dogs for their seventh birthday.

   b. The neighbors noticed that Stephanie and Becky did a great job training their own dogs.

   c. Stephanie and Becky sent out flyers to advertise their business.

   d. Stephanie and Becky started a successful dog training business.

5. What does "ringing off the hook" mean?

   a. The phone was ringing all the time.

   b. The phone fell off a hook that it was hanging on.

   c. The ringing of the phone sounded like a hook.

   d. A hook made the phone ring.

Windy Canyon Middle School

Bulletin for December 17

- Remember that Friday, December 21, is the last day of school before the holiday break. It is also teacher conference day, so the school will be in session only until 12:30 p.m.

- The fourth, fifth, and sixth graders will be presenting "Celebrations of the Season" on Wednesday, December 19 at 7:00 p.m. Admission to the show is free. Bring your whole family for some fun and lively holiday spirit!

- Mrs. Bowman had a baby girl on Sunday at 3:00 a.m. The baby weighs eight pounds, three ounces and is named Shakira June. Congratulations to the parents and their new daughter!

- Our librarian, Ms. Nelson, reminds everyone that reading a book is a great way to spend the holiday break. Come on in to the library. Ms. Nelson will be glad to recommend some of her favorite titles.

- Mr. Henderson will be presenting a science fair in March. Anyone who is interested in participating should see Mr. Henderson in room 23 to sign up.

- The Public Library Book Talkers are coming this week! Angie will be visiting rooms 24, 25, and 29 tomorrow. Mark will be visiting rooms 7, 10, and 12 on Thursday. Don't forget to bring your library cards! Only students with library cards will be allowed to check out books. Angie says she has some super-exciting choices this time, so be prepared!

- Tony D'Agostino lost a blue parka yesterday in the cafeteria. Has anyone found it? Please bring it to the office if you have. He is very cold without it.

- There are rumors that the Poetry Squad will be roving through classrooms today. Keep your eyes and ears open!

- Lunch today will be sloppy joes, french fries, green beans, and frosted brownies. Yum!

Our Windy Canyon Middle School Hunger Drive has collected over 2,500 cans of food so far! We want to express our many thanks to everyone who has participated. We will be dropping the cans off at the local homeless shelter Friday evening. This will help many families have a happier holiday season!

Windy Canyon Middle School *(cont.)*

1. Which of the following is in a form that could be posted in this bulletin?

   a. Reading, math, science, lunch, physical education, social studies

   b. After-School Enrichment classes begin on Thursday, January 17.

   c. The capital of the United States is Washington, D.C.

   d. The chairs in the cafeteria are orange and yellow plastic.

2. What would a Public Library Book Talker most likely say to a class?

   a. "Thank you for all the cans of food you have donated!"

   b. "Be sure to sign up for the March Science Fair."

   c. "If you like adventure stories, you'll love *Missing in the Mountains!*"

   d. "Remember the sing-along after 'Celebrations of the Season.'"

3. Why will Ms. Nelson recommend some good books?

   a. She wants the library empty so that she can clean it more easily.

   b. She wants students to be prepared so they can talk to Angie when she visits.

   c. She wants people to buy books so she can donate the money to the Hunger Drive.

   d. She wants students to do something both fun and educational over school vacation.

4. Why is there an announcement about Tony D'Agostino?

   a. He wants to find his lost coat because it is cold outside.

   b. He is selling frosted brownies for teacher conference day.

   c. His mother just had a baby, and he is proud of his new sister.

   d. He is helping Mr. Henderson organize the science fair.

5. Which of the following is an example of an opinion?

   a. Admission to the holiday show is free.

   b. The Public Library Book Talkers are coming this week!

   c. Mr. Henderson will be presenting a science fair in March.

   d. Angie has some super-exciting choices this time.

Sentence Structure

One way to improve the quality of your paragraphs is to combine short, simple sentences.

Example: Jarrod was beside us. Jake was beside us. We did not know they were even in the house.

Jarrod and Jake were beside us before we knew they were even in the house.

Another way to make your sentences more interesting is to move around the parts of your sentences so they do not always start the same way, with the subject, for example.

Example: Before we knew they were even in the house, Jarrod and Jake were beside us.

Improve the sentences in the following paragraph by combining short, simple ones and by moving around the parts of the sentences so they do not always start the same way. (You may also change the order of the sentences and add or remove specific details.)

Trees Bear Gifts

Trees give us many things. Trees give us shade on hot days. Trees give us wood with which to build our homes. Trees give us fruit to eat. Trees give us leaves we can use for mulch. Trees provide shelter for the birds and other animals we enjoy. Trees give shelter from the rain. Trees can be good places to hide.
Trees can be good places to play. Trees give us a place to build tree houses. Trees are also beautiful to look at. Trees may stay green all year long. Trees may lose all their leaves in the fall and winter.

Identifying Sentences

Declarative sentences make statements: *I like ice cream.*

Imperative sentences make requests or give commands: *Buy me some ice cream.*

Interrogative sentences ask questions: *Should I get one scoop or two?*

Exclamatory sentences (which are often short sentences) express strong feeling: *This ice cream is fantastic!*

(*Helpful Hint:* End punctuation for declarative and imperative sentences is the period. Interrogative sentences end with question marks, and exclamatory sentences end with exclamation points.)

Label the following sentences **D** (declarative), **IP** (imperative), **IT** (interrogative), or **E** (exclamatory).

1. _____ Yesterday Rosa, Lucille, Ricardo, and Luke went to the Uptown Mall to shop for clothes.

2. _____ Do you think this olive green shirt looks good on me?

3. _____ Let's buy it right now!

4. _____ Go to the salesperson and tell her you want to buy it.

5. _____ Where is she?

6. _____ I don't see anyone around here who is a salesperson.

7. _____ Perhaps they are all at lunch and there is no one here to sell things to us.

8. _____ That is impossible!

9. _____ Oh, look at this!

10. _____ This is the most beautiful jacket I have ever seen, Rosa.

11. _____ Lucille, I think you should buy it.

12. _____ But I don't want to buy a jacket unless Ricardo is also going to get one.

13. _____ That's silly!

14. _____ Okay, I will buy the jacket.

15. _____ Where did that salesperson go?

What is a Subject?

A sentence is a group of words that tell about something. A sentence tells about a person, place, or thing doing something. Here is a sentence.

The   boy   ran.

Who is this sentence about? The sentence is about the boy. The subject of the sentence is the boy. A subject of a sentence is who or what the sentence is about.

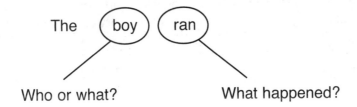

Who or what?   What happened?

Read the following sentences and see if you can find the subject of each sentence. Who or what is the sentence about? Circle the subject in each sentence.

1. The school was given the top rating.

2. The dog is attending obedience school.

3. The sun set on the horizon.

4. First graders love to read.

5. Spring is coming.

Look at the subjects below. Write sentences using each of these subjects. Remember, the sentence must be about these subjects.

6. Lisa

_____

7. zoo

_____

8. peanuts

_____

9. bicycle

_____

10. airplane

_____

What is the Predicate?

Just as all sentences have a subject, they also have a predicate. A predicate tells important things about the subject. The predicate tells what the subject does, has, or is. In the sentence below, the word *ran* is the predicate. It explains what the *boy*, the subject, is doing.

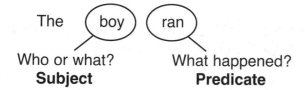

The (boy) (ran)

Who or what?   What happened?
Subject   **Predicate**

Draw a circle around the subject in the sentences below. Once you have located the subject in each of the sentences, underline the predicate. The first one has been done for you.

1. The (dog) jumped into the lake.

2. Everyone was laughing.

3. Erika has a cold.

4. The cat jumped off the log.

5. They ate the birthday cake.

6. She can do a backward flip.

7. Summer is the time for fishing.

Write sentences using the following predicates:

8. jumped into the water _____

9. claps at the end _____

10. eats hot dogs _____

11. races the boys _____

12. is happy _____

13. sits on the bench _____

14. always eats ketchup _____

Sentence Building

Fill in the boxes below to form a complete sentence. For example: *The caterpillar smiled.   An ugly frog jumped along the bank just now.*

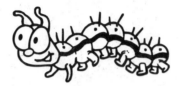

article	noun	verb
		(Did what?)
	(caterpillar)	
subject		**predicate**

article	noun	verb
		(Did what?)
	(seal)	
subject		**predicate**

70

Sentence Building *(cont.)*

article	adjective	noun	verb (Did what?)	(Where?)	(When?)
		(frog)			
subject			**predicate**		

article	adjective	noun	verb (Did what?)	(Where?)	(When?)
		(otter)			
subject			**predicate**		

Tone

Tone in a composition is the feeling that is expressed by the writer through choice of topic and through word choice throughout the paragraph or essay. The tone can be one of anger, sorrow, excitement, humor, or happiness—any emotion that the writer wants to convey.

Read each group of sentences below. Then write the tone each group of sentences expresses. Choose from the words in the box. Use each word only once.

happy	excited	funny	worried	sad

1. Wow! Today is my birthday. I know it will be a great day. We are having a chocolate cake, and we are going to play games. I can hardly wait until all my friends arrive to help me celebrate my special day.

   Tone: _____

2. I can't believe my best friend is moving away. I want to cry. Even the sky looks gray and rainy today. Nothing will ever be the same again without my friend to share things with.

   Tone: _____

3. Can a pig learn tricks? My pet pig, Sally, can roll over and shake hands. Maybe I should say she can shake pig's feet. She is a funny pig who really likes to "hog the show."

   Tone: _____

4. I cannot believe that our arithmetic test is today. I forgot to study, and I do not understand multiplication. I just know I will fail this test. This could ruin my math grade. Oh, why didn't I study last night?

   Tone: _____

5. It is an absolutely beautiful day today! The sun is shining, the birds are singing, and the air smells sweet and fresh. It feels good to be alive!

   Tone: _____

Who Is Talking?
Identifying Voice

Read the paragraphs below and write the type of person you think is talking in that paragraph. Describe the age of the person, if they are male or female, even what type of job you think they might have.

Sample Paragraph #1

We now have a cement slab for the new house next door to us. I suspect tomorrow will be the day they begin putting up the sides and rafters. It has been interesting to watch all the steps from our kitchen window. Last Friday when the slab was poured, it took at least eight fellows, maybe more.

Who is talking?_____

Sample Paragraph #2

I feel violence is a problem because of the effect it has on ordinary people. I don't understand how people can be so ignorant, how they can do such mean things to other people. It is scary when you hear on the news how somebody has killed seven people. There should be harsh punishments for such things. Sometimes I think the death penalty is not even enough.

Who is talking?_____

Sample Paragraph #3

So, how's it going? Were you a little scared on the first day of school? I was a little bit curious but not really scared. My border on my name tag was really terrific. I just wish the teacher had spelled my name right. But what can you expect with a name like Flingenbocher? I wish I had a name like yours, Hill.

Who is talking?_____

Segues and Transitions

Segues and transitions are used to connect thoughts and ideas. The chart below contains a list of common segues and transitions.

above	consequently	moreover
according to	even though	nevertheless
additionally	for instance	next
after	furthermore	obviously
along with	however	of course
also	in addition to	similarly
although	in conclusion	since
another	in fact	therefore
as a result	in summary	to emphasize
because	last	while
besides	lastly	yet
clearly	likewise	meanwhile

Read the following sentences and notice the segues and transitions being used. Notice how they enhance the sentences. Note the comma use as well in some of the sentences.

1. **Consequently**, the director decided to add more woodwind instruments.

2. **Meanwhile**, the audience was left stunned by what just happened on stage.

3. **Obviously**, the students had practiced their instruments quite a bit.

4. **Clearly**, the parents of the soloist must be very proud.

5. **As a result** of reading the first book, I knew what to expect.

Now, write your own sentences using at least one segue or transition in each sentence.

1. _____

2. _____

3. _____

4. _____

5. _____

6. _____

74

Use Imagery: Similes

A **simile** is a direct comparison between two unrelated things. A simile shows how the two things are alike in one special way. The words *like* or *as* are used to make the comparison.

Example: Oliver swims *like* a fish.

The phrases below are the beginnings of similes. Complete each one, making a sentence. You may add more than one word.

1. Our lazy cat sleeps like _____.

2. The hospital emergency room was as busy as _____.

3. Autumn leaves are falling just like _____.

4. On my birthday, I am as happy as _____.

5. The leftover meatloaf tasted like _____.

6. After work, Mother is as hungry as a _____.

Create similes of your own to describe the following:

1. the color of the sunset _____.

2. the feeling you have on the first day of school _____.

3. a butterfly on its way south _____.

4. the way a newborn puppy feels in your hands _____.

Sense Matrix

Below is a sense matrix that has been filled in for two different objects, a potato chip and an ice cube. In the blank matrix, think of three more objects and fill in the appropriate spaces with descriptive words.

Sense Matrix

Object	Appearance	Feels	Smells	Tastes	Sounds
potato chip	curved, fried, ridged, spoon-like, yellowish	gritty, rough, greasy	tangy tempting	salty crunchy	crunch
ice cube	square, dense, 3-D, white, melting	cold wet slippery smooth	fresh brisk cool	wet-like cold water	crackling dripping

Sense Matrix

Object	Appearance	Feels	Smells	Tastes	Sounds

Paragraph Maze Game

Find your way through the maze by making a paragraph. Some words in the paragraph are written right to left and bottom to top, so read carefully!

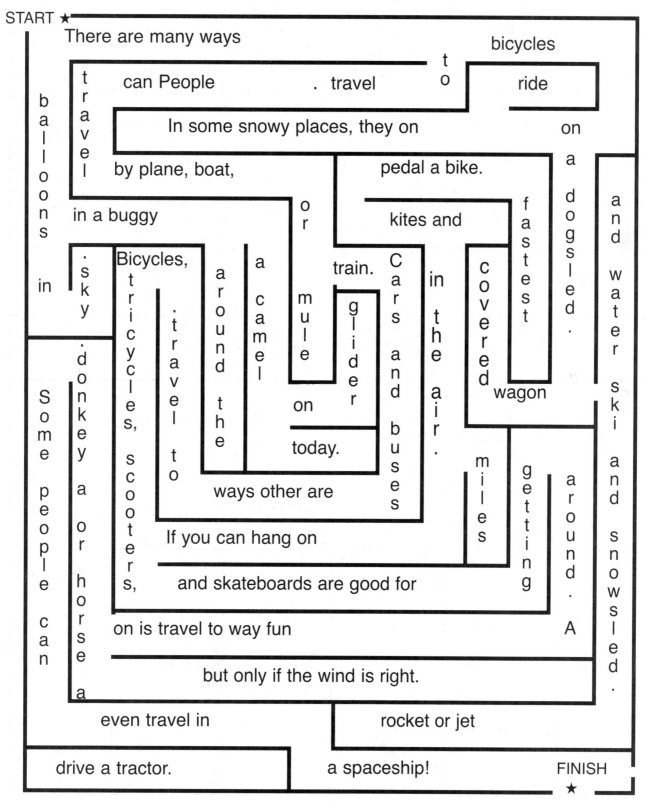

Choose a Topic and List Ideas

A paragraph should be about a single, narrow topic. After you choose a topic, you make a list of ideas or details to use when writing about that topic.

In the box is a list of six topics about which you might choose to write. Below the box are six idea lists. First, write the correct topic above each list of ideas or details. Then add one idea to each list.

good friends	**Thanksgiving**	**pets**
movies	**wintertime**	**exercise**

1. **Topic:** _____

- a time family comes together

- most delicious meal of the year

- reminder of how fortunate we are

- _____

2. **Topic:** _____

- like adventure best of all

- don't like mushy romances

- prefer to go to matinees

- _____

3. **Topic:** _____

- favorite pastime is skiing

- also like to go ice skating

- inside, reading by the fire

- _____

4. **Topic:** _____

- keeps a secret

- goes camping with me

- lets me borrow clothes

- _____

5. **Topic:** _____

- favorite is walking

- jogging hard on my knees

- prefer to be outside

- _____

6. **Topic:** _____

- teach responsibility

- reward owner with love

- dog is the best

- _____

Beginning: Topic Sentence

The topic sentence is the guide for the rest of the paragraph. It lets the reader know exactly what the paragraph is about. Every detail used must refer to the content of the topic sentence.

- Create a topic sentence for each main idea or topic below.
- Two spaces have been left blank so that you can write your own topics and the topic sentences to go with them.

1. school band

_____

2. my neighborhood

_____

3. my family

_____

4. spring

_____

5. importance of music

_____

6. best vacation spot

_____

7. computer uses

_____

8. _____

_____

9. _____

_____

Middle: Body Sentences

Body sentences or supporting details expand the topic sentence. They help make the topic or main idea clearer and give significant information about it.

- Choose one of the topics from the previous page, one you added or one of the others, for which you can develop supporting details.
- Write the topic sentence.
- On the lines below the topic sentence, write at least six sentences that are details that give specific information about your topic sentence. (Your choice of topic will be decided by the number of supporting details you can think of.)

topic sentence

_____

_____

body sentences

_____

_____

_____

_____

_____

_____

_____

End: Concluding Sentence

The final sentence of a paragraph is the closing or concluding sentence. It comes at the end of the supporting details or the body of the paragraph. The conclusion should express the feeling, attitude, or point of the paragraph.

Add concluding sentences to the following paragraphs.

My family's new house is a very comfortable place to be. One thing that makes it so comfortable is that I now have a room of my own and do not have to share with my messy younger brother. Another thing is that the temperature is more even because of the new construction. Best of all, we now have a kitchen that is big enough for a table and chairs, so we can have our family meals there. That means I usually don't have to worry about spilling things on the dining room carpet when I eat.

concluding sentence: _____

_____

Geraldine, my older sister, can be a really big nuisance. Her main fault is that she cannot mind her own business. If one of my friends comes to visit for the afternoon or to stay overnight, we never have any privacy. For some reason, Geraldine seems to think that she should supervise us. If we are sitting in my room listening to music or watching television, she will come in without being asked and check to see, I guess, that we are not doing anything that she thinks we should not be doing.

concluding sentence:_____

_____

Revise, Edit, and Proofread the Paragraph

Use the following checklist to revise, edit, and proofread your paragraph. Then, write and proofread the final copy of your paragraph.

Essay Checklist

1. _____ Add specific details where development is needed.

2. _____ Remove details not directly related to the topic.

3. _____ Vary sentence structure. Combine sentences. Change the order of sentences.

4. _____ Use exact words and add descriptive words—nouns, verbs, adjectives, adverbs.

5. _____ Use figurative language—similes and metaphors.

6. _____ Check for consistent tone throughout the essay.

7. _____ Correct fragments and run-on sentences.

8. _____ Use transition words.

9. _____ Check grammar.

10. _____ Check capitalization.

11. _____ Check punctuation.

12. _____ Check spelling.

Editing and Rewriting Activities

Editing is the last stage before rewriting a paper for publication. Careful attention is given to removing grammatical and spelling errors. Use the chart below to help you edit your paragraph for spelling and grammatical mistakes.

Proofreading Marks

Editor's Mark	Meaning	Example
≡	capitalize	they fished in lake tahoe.
/	make it lower case	Five Students missed the Bus.
SP	spelling mistake	The day was clowdy and cold.
⊙	add a period	Tomorrow is a holiday ⊙
⸜	delete (remove)	One person knew the the answer.
∧	add a word	Six were in the litter.
⸜⸝	add a comma	He planted peas corn, and squash.
∿	reverse words or letters	An otter swam in the bed kelp.
ⱽ	add an apostrophe	The child s bike was red.
ⱽ ⱽ	add quotation marks	Why can't I go? she cried.
#	make a space	He ate two redapples.
⌒	close the space	Her favorite game is soft ball.
¶	begin a new paragraph	to know. Next on the list

Write an Expository Paragraph

Make a plan for writing a paragraph to explain how to do something, or give facts or directions. Plan your paragraph:

- Choose a topic.

- Develop a topic sentence.

- Make a list of supporting details to develop into body sentences.

- Compose a concluding sentence.

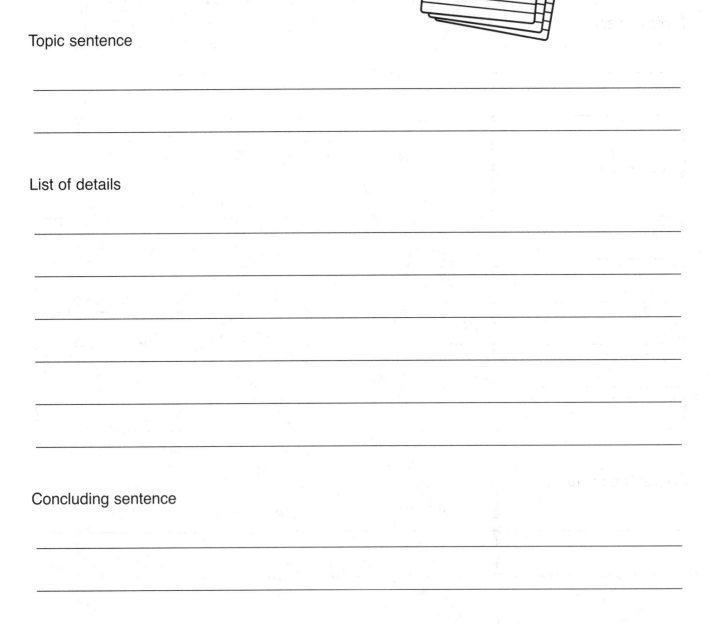

Topic sentence

_____

_____

List of details

_____

_____

_____

_____

_____

Concluding sentence

_____

_____

84

Write a Narrative Paragraph

Make a plan for writing about an experience or an event. Plan your paragraph:

- Choose a topic.
- Develop a topic sentence.
- Make a list of supporting details to develop into body sentences.
- Compose a concluding sentence.

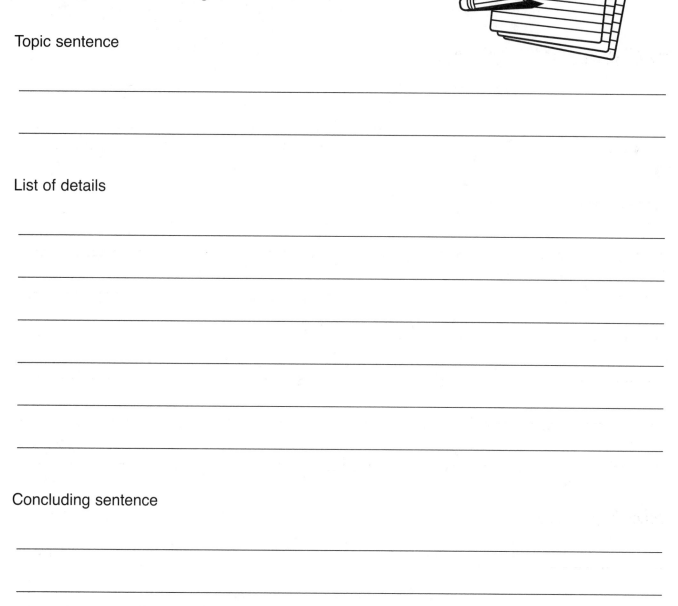

Topic sentence

_____

_____

List of details

_____

_____

_____

_____

_____

Concluding sentence

_____

_____

Write a Friendly Letter

Make a plan for writing a letter to a friend. Your friend may live nearby or far away. Plan your friendly letter:

- Respond to letters you have received in the past.
- Tell about your most recent activities.
- Report any special news.
- Refer to any mutual friends and/or your family.

Response to previous correspondence

_____

_____

Most recent activities

_____

_____

_____

Special news

_____

_____

_____

Mutual friends, family

_____

_____

Write a Friendly Letter *(cont.)*

Write a letter to a friend and address an envelope to send it in. Don't forget to put on a stamp before you mail it. Use the form on this page to compose your letter.

_____
(your address)

_____

_____
(today's date)

_____
(greeting)

_____

_____

_____

_____

_____

_____

_____

_____

_____

_____
(closing)

_____
(your name)

Persuasive or Editorial Writing

When writing an opinion or editorial, follow the format below:

Guidelines

1. Choose a topic for your writing.

2. Give a detailed description of the problem or issue in paragraph one.

3. In paragraph two, tell the reader why this issue or problem is important to consider or think about.

4. Tell what the solution should be and write the benefits of your solution in paragraph three.

Example:

No More Homework for 4th Graders

There should be a law made that states children in the fourth grade should no longer be required to do homework. Homework is very boring. Kids should not have to do any of it at all. This issue needs to be addressed because children everywhere have homework on weeknights when they go to school.

It is very important to cancel homework for all fourth-grade students at this time because they are very busy with other things in life. They have friends. They have chores, clubs, and sports. Homework takes a lot of time. If fourth graders didn't have homework, they would be much happier students.

The best solution to this problem in the United States is to pass a law that bans homework for all fourth graders. Teachers need to be told they cannot give homework. There need to be police who make sure no one is getting homework in the fourth grade. If a person breaks the law, he or she should be put in jail.

The things that would happen if there were laws to ban homework would be terrific! All fourth graders would have more time to play after school. They would have more time for friends. They would be happier and give their parents less trouble. Lastly, they would fight with their parents less because there would be no reason to fight with them. Let's get rid of homework!

Use the guidelines to help you create a fantastic opinion essay or editorial of your own. You may write on the back of this paper.

_____

_____

_____

_____

Description of an Essay and Sample Topics

An essay consists of a series of paragraphs. The basic structure of the essay is the same as the structure of a paragraph:

- The topic sentence of the paragraph becomes an introductory paragraph.

- The main body sentences of the paragraph are each developed into separate paragraphs to become the body of the essay.

- The concluding sentence becomes a fully developed concluding paragraph.

Also, just as there are expository, narrative, comparison/contrast and persuasive paragraphs, there are expository, narrative, comparison/contrast and persuasive essays.

The following is a sample outline for a paragraph:

I. **topic sentence**—I would like very much to have my very own dog.

II. **supporting details**—There are three reasons I think I should have my own dog.

   A. **first reason**—The one dog we have seems to belong more to my older brother.

   B. **second reason**—Both of us cannot go to different places with Buster at the same time.

   C. **third reason**—I think that it is just as important for me to have a pet that is my companion as it is for my brother to have one.

III. **concluding sentence**—For these reasons, I think that I should be allowed to have a dog.

This paragraph outline can easily be expanded into an outline for an essay. Each supporting detail can be developed into a paragraph by giving more details about it and by using examples. On the next page is an expansion of the above paragraph outline into an essay outline.

Description of an Essay and Sample Topics *(cont.)*

The following is an example of an outline of an essay:

I. Introduction—I would like very much to have my very own dog.

  A. The dog we have now came into our family before I was born.

  B. Buster was friends with my older brother before he ever knew me.

II. Body—There are three reasons I think I should have my own dog.

  A. Buster seems to belong to my older brother.

    1. He always goes to Jerry first.

    2. If my brother starts to leave the house, Buster always wants to go with him.

  B. Both of us cannot go to different places at the same time with Buster.

    1. It seems that every time I want to take Buster with me for a walk, Jerry has already left to take Buster somewhere else.

    2. When I am home alone, I would like to have a dog who is loyal to only me.

  C. I think it is just as important for me to have a pet as it is for Jerry to have one.

    1. Just as Jerry has, I can learn to be responsible for a pet.

    2. Just as Jerry has one, I could have my own loyal companion.

III. Conclusion—Therefore, I think it would be a good idea for me to have my own dog.

  A. I would have a pet to care for and one to care for me.

  B. The dog would get to know me from the beginning and be my loyal companion.

On the next page, write a topic and some ideas for your essay. Then choose one of the graphic organizers on pages 92–96 to help you plan your essay.

Choose an Essay Topic and List Ideas

You may write about any topic you choose, and you may write any kind of essay you choose.

That means you may write an expository essay in which you explain how to do something. You may write a narrative essay in which you tell a story about some event in your life. You may write an essay in which you give your opinions about a subject and try to persuade your reader to agree with you. You may write a comparison/contrast essay pointing out the similarities and differences between two people or things.

Choose a topic for your essay.

Topic _____

Write down all the ideas you can think of that you could use to develop and support your topic. Think of examples, incidents, reasons—all the details that you could possibly use to support your essay topic.

List your ideas: _____

_____

_____

_____

_____

_____

_____

_____

_____

Make Me a Cheese Sandwich

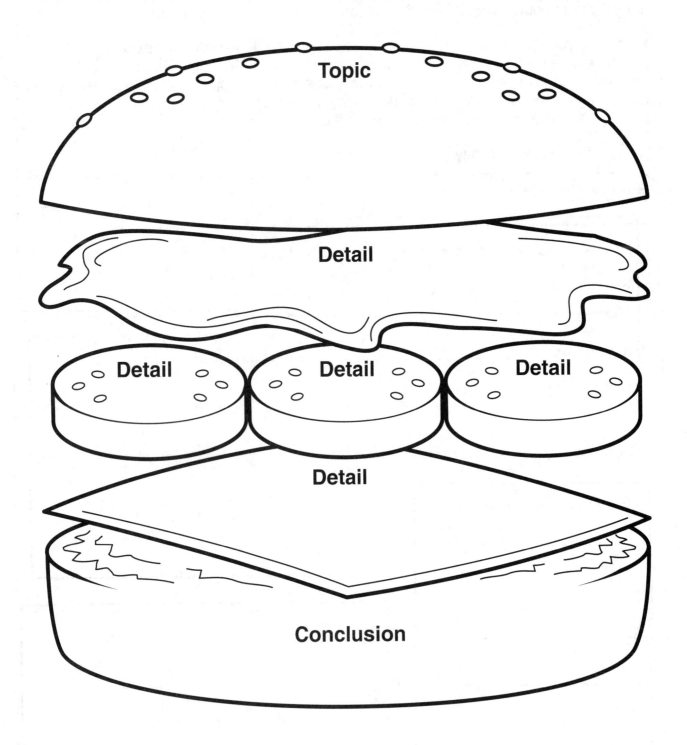

Topic

Detail

Detail   Detail   Detail

Detail

Conclusion

92

A Map to Organization

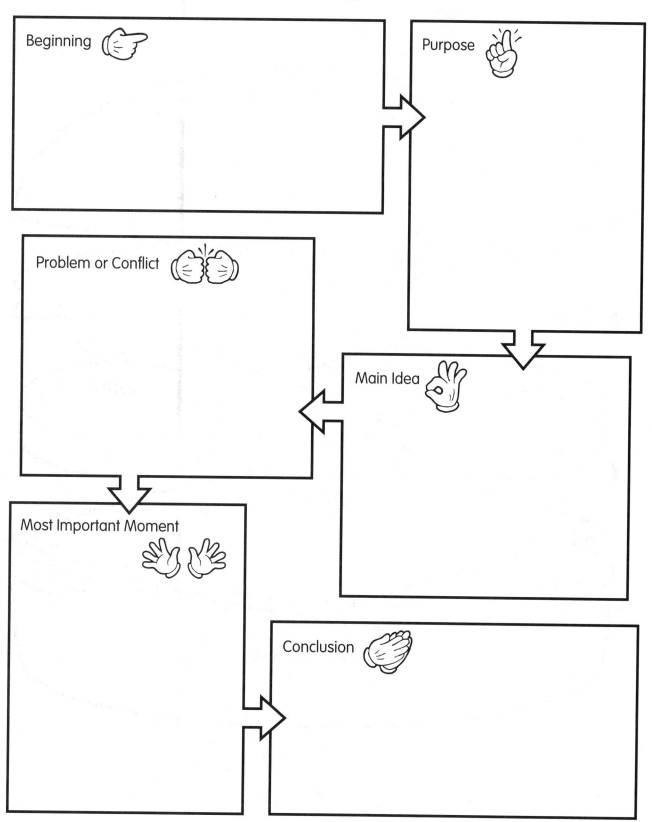

Beginning

Purpose

Problem or Conflict

Main Idea

Most Important Moment

Conclusion

Herringbone

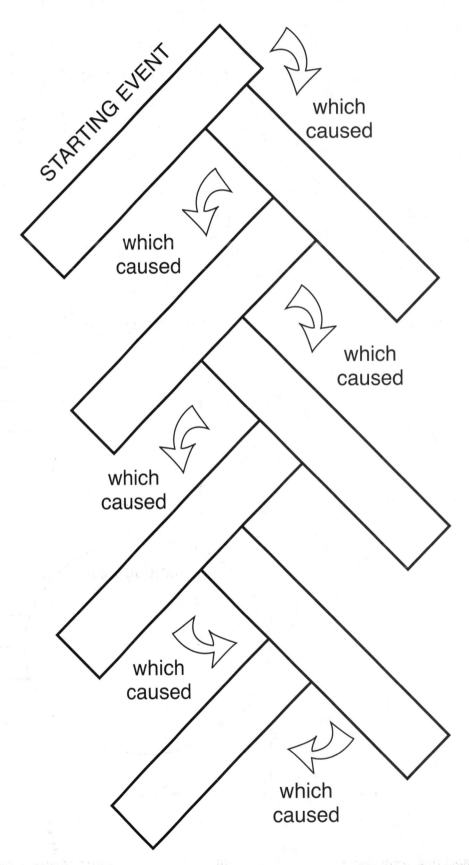

STARTING EVENT

which
caused

which
caused

which
caused

which
caused

which
caused

which
caused

94

Essay Graphic Organizer

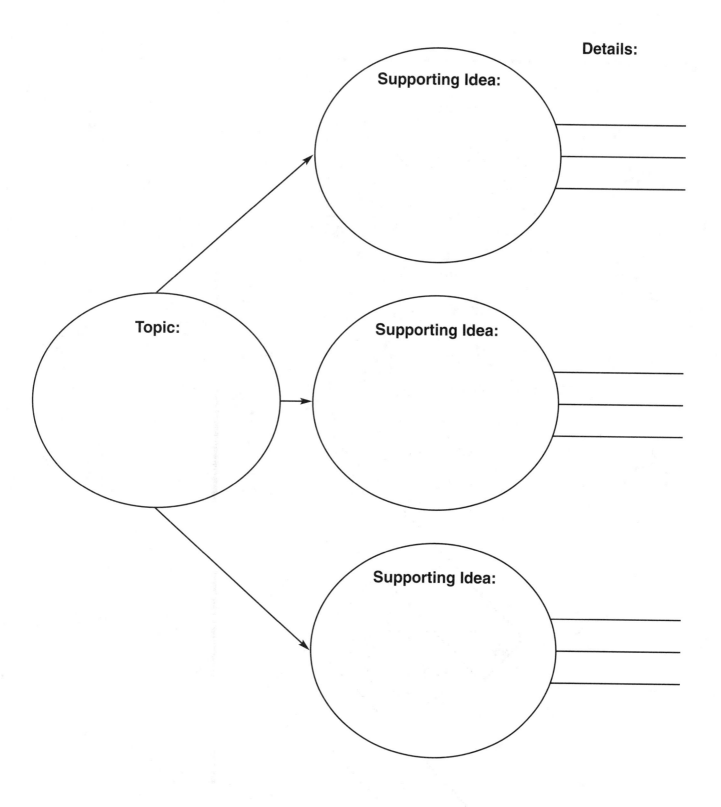

Details:

Supporting Idea:

Topic:

Supporting Idea:

Supporting Idea:

Story Map

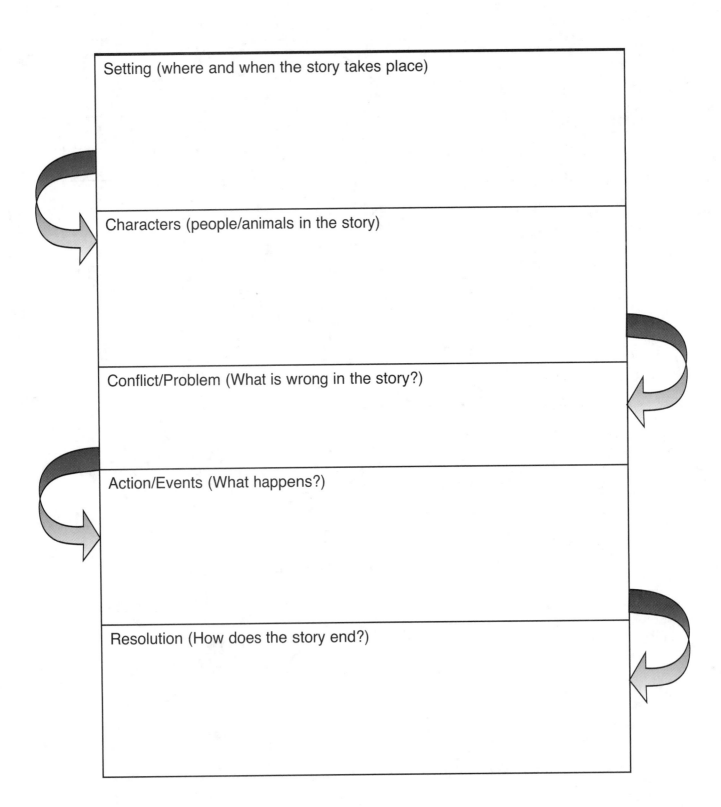

Setting (where and when the story takes place)

Characters (people/animals in the story)

Conflict/Problem (What is wrong in the story?)

Action/Events (What happens?)

Resolution (How does the story end?)

Assessment: Develop an Essay

- Add a conclusion to the topic sentence and list of ideas that you composed on page 91.

- Write the complete essay below.

- Add a title that is based on the content of the topic sentence of your essay.

_____

_____

_____

_____

_____

_____

_____

_____

_____

_____

_____

Missing Numbers: Addition

Directions: Write the missing number, represented by the square, on the line below the number sentence.

1. $9 + 8 = \square$

_____

2. $10 + 27 = \square$

_____

3. $16 + 23 = \square$

_____

4. $60 + 31 = \square$

_____

5. $9 + \square = 21$

_____

6. $\square + 11 = 31$

_____

7. $13 + \square = 40$

_____

8. $\square + 6 = 24$

_____

9. $\square + 10 = 52$

_____

10. $25 + \square = 50$

_____

11. $\square + 13 = 20$

_____

12. $8 + \square = 22$

_____

13. $6 + \square = 29$

_____

14. $\square + 9 = 31$

_____

15. $\square + 11 = 20$

_____

16. $11 + \square = 47$

_____

17. $19 + \square = 69$

_____

18. $\square + 12 = 48$

_____

19. $21 + \square = 100$

_____

20. $\square + 13 = 64$

_____

21. $\square + 33 = 66$

_____

22. $15 + \square = 55$

_____

23. $16 + \square = 30$

_____

24. $\square + 29 = 36$

_____

How Much?

32 dollars

26 dollars

64 dollars

49 dollars

57 dollars

17 dollars

Use the prices to write addition problems. Find the sums.

a. 1 ⬡ + 1 👞 =

___ + ___ = ___

d. 1 👖 + 1 👞 =

___ + ___ = ___

b. 1 👗 + 1 👖 =

___ + ___ = ___

e. 1 ⌚ + 1 🎩 + 1 ⬡ =

___ + ___ + ___ = ___

c. 1 🎩 + 1 ⌚ =

___ + ___ = ___

f. 1 👗 + 1 👞 + 1 👖 =

___ + ___ + ___ = ___

Adding 2-Digit Numbers

Read each word problem. Write the number sentence it shows. Find the sum.

1. In the forest, Lisa counted 83 pine trees, 24 spider webs, and 16 chipmunks. How many things did she count in all?

_____ + _____ + _____ = _____

2. In Bill's classroom there are 47 pencils, 21 pieces of chalk, and 33 bottles of glue. How many supplies are there in all?

_____ + _____ + _____ = _____

3. At the park, Carla counted 14 ducks, 32 children, and 24 roller skates. How many things did she count in all?

_____ + _____ + _____ = _____

4. James counted 36 stars one night, 42 stars the next, and 87 on the third night. How many stars did he count in all?

_____ + _____ + _____ = _____

Name That Cartoon!

In 1928, Walt Disney released his first animated cartoon. What was the name of that cartoon? To discover the answer, find the sum for each one of the math problems. Write the letter that matches each sum on the line.

1. 2,546 + 6,766 A	2. 3,172 + 9,512 B	3. 3,892 + 1,010 E	4. 1,346 + 1,610 I	5. 9,881 + 7,545 L
6. 2,110 + 8,794 M	7. 9,734 + 7,132 O	8. 5,510 + 4,682 S	9. 8,393 + 4,931 T	10. 5,851 + 6,278 W

____ ____ ____ ____ ____ ____ ____ ____ ____
10,192 13,324 4,902 9,312 10,904 12,684 16,866 9,312 13,324

____ ____ ____ ____ ____ ____
12,129 2,956 17,426 17,426 2,956 4,902

Wheels-R-Us

Use the chart to answer the questions.

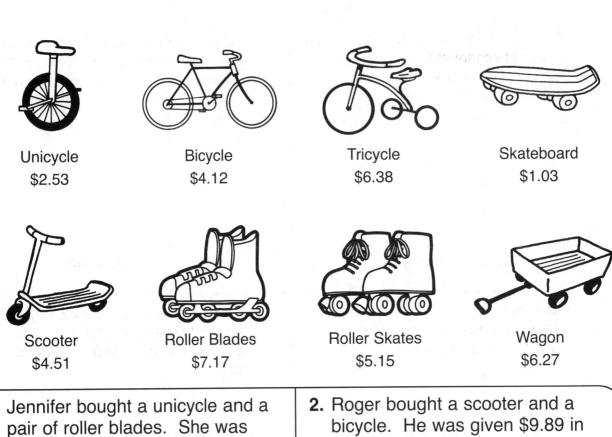

Unicycle $2.53	Bicycle $4.12	Tricycle $6.38	Skateboard $1.03
Scooter $4.51	Roller Blades $7.17	Roller Skates $5.15	Wagon $6.27

1. Jennifer bought a unicycle and a pair of roller blades. She was given $9.65 in change. How much money did Jennifer have?

Jennifer had _____ .

2. Roger bought a scooter and a bicycle. He was given $9.89 in change. How much money did Roger have?

Roger had _____ .

3. Simon bought a tricycle and a scooter. He was given $4.84 in change. How much money did Simon have?

Simon had _____ .

4. Irene bought a skateboard and a wagon. She was given $8.46 in change. How much money did Irene have?

Irene had _____ .

5. Susan bought a wagon, a unicycle, and a scooter. She was given $0.38 in change. How much money did she have?

Susan had _____ .

6. Amit bought a pair of roller blades, a tricycle, and a skateboard. He was given $0.36 in change. How much money did he have?

Amit had _____ .

Telling Time Differences

Solve each word problem.

1. Dale leaves for school at 9:10 A.M. He arrives at school at 9:32 A.M. How many minutes does it take Dale to walk to school?

_____ minutes

2. Regina put the cookies in the oven at 9:20 A.M. She took the cookies out at 9:37 A.M. How many minutes did the cookies bake?

_____ minutes

3. Edna began playing the piano at 10:10 A.M. and finished at 10:45 A.M. How long did Edna practice?

_____ minutes

4. Garrett started cleaning the tub at 2:44 P.M. and finished at 2:59 P.M. How long did it take Garrett to clean the tub?

_____ minutes

5. Tobias left the library at 2:10 P.M. and arrived back home at 2:55 P.M. How long did it take Tobias to walk home?

_____ minutes

6. Ruby left for the mall at 6:41 P.M. and reached the mall at 7:20 P.M. How long did it take Ruby to walk to the mall?

_____ minutes

Adding and Subtracting 3-Digit Numbers

Solve each problem. Show your work.

1. Old MacDonald has 379 sheep, 108 pigs, and 135 chickens. How many animals are there in all?

   There are _____ animals in all.

2. Old MacDonald has 912 bulls and 516 cows. How many more bulls than cows are there?

   There are _____ more bulls than cows.

3. Old MacDonald has 298 goats and 187 kids (baby goats). How many more goats than kids are there?

   There are _____ more goats than kids.

4. Old MacDonald's children have pets. The children have 154 cats, 152 dogs, and 315 mice. How many pets are there in all?

   There are _____ pets in all.

5. Old MacDonald has 733 bales of hay. He fed 279 of the bales of hay to the horses. How many bales of hay are left?

   There are _____ bales of hay left.

6. Old MacDonald has 108 horses in the barn, 693 horses in the pasture, and 160 horses rounding up the cows. How many horses are there in all?

   There are _____ horses in all.

7. Which animal does Old MacDonald have the most of?_____

8. Which animal does Old MacDonald have the fewest of? _____

9. Which one of Old MacDonald's animals has only 2 legs?_____

10. Are there more pets or more horses? _____

Adding and Subtracting 5-and-6-Digit Numbers

Solve each word problem. Show your work.

1. Hope gathered 56,329 pounds of walnuts and 10,428 pounds of pecans. How many pounds of nuts did Hope gather in all?

   Hope gathered _____ pounds of nuts in all.

2. Godfrey picked 34,159 pounds of corn and 11,724 pounds of peas. How many pounds of vegetables did Godfrey gather in all?

   Godfrey gathered _____ pounds of vegetables in all.

3. Mom earned 573,319 frequent flier miles. Dad earned 421,569 frequent flier miles. How many frequent flier miles did they earn in all?

   They earned _____ frequent flier miles in all.

4. Grandma has traveled 765,863 miles. Grandpa has traveled 134,018 miles. How many miles have they traveled in all?

   They have traveled _____ miles in all.

5. Jim Brown rushed for 12,312 yards. Franco Harris rushed 12,120 yards. How many more yards did Jim Brown rush?

   Jim Brown rushed _____ more yards.

6. A doctor earns $59,300 a year while a secretary earns $20,600 a year. How much more does a doctor earn?

   A doctor earns _____ more.

Estimating Differences

Estimate the differences by rounding each number to the nearest hundred and then subtracting. Circle your answer.

1. There are 323 jumbo jets and 187 puddle jumpers. What is the difference?

about 100

about 200

about 300

2. There are 258 first-class tickets and 814 coach tickets. What is the difference?

about 300

about 400

about 500

3. There are 312 chicken dinners and 439 fish dinners. What is the difference?

about 0

about 100

about 200

4. There are 110 business people and 942 families on the plane. What is the difference?

about 800

about 900

about 1,000

5. There are 976 passengers and 626 window seats. What is the difference?

about 300

about 400

about 500

6. Two hundred fifty-one planes departed late and 662 planes departed on time. What is the difference?

about 200

about 300

about 400

Find the Difference

Find the differences.

a. $\begin{array}{r} 31 \\ -\ 23 \\ \hline \end{array}$	**g.** $\begin{array}{r} 79 \\ -\ 32 \\ \hline \end{array}$	**m.** $\begin{array}{r} 85 \\ -\ 21 \\ \hline \end{array}$	**s.** $\begin{array}{r} 69 \\ -\ 37 \\ \hline \end{array}$
b. $\begin{array}{r} 75 \\ -\ 42 \\ \hline \end{array}$	**h.** $\begin{array}{r} 57 \\ -\ 51 \\ \hline \end{array}$	**n.** $\begin{array}{r} 51 \\ -\ 20 \\ \hline \end{array}$	**t.** $\begin{array}{r} 98 \\ -\ 34 \\ \hline \end{array}$
c. $\begin{array}{r} 54 \\ -\ 23 \\ \hline \end{array}$	**i.** $\begin{array}{r} 88 \\ -\ 44 \\ \hline \end{array}$	**o.** $\begin{array}{r} 42 \\ -\ 28 \\ \hline \end{array}$	**u.** $\begin{array}{r} 87 \\ -\ 28 \\ \hline \end{array}$
d. $\begin{array}{r} 42 \\ -\ 26 \\ \hline \end{array}$	**j.** $\begin{array}{r} 63 \\ -\ 23 \\ \hline \end{array}$	**p.** $\begin{array}{r} 71 \\ -\ 56 \\ \hline \end{array}$	**v.** $\begin{array}{r} 69 \\ -\ 43 \\ \hline \end{array}$
e. $\begin{array}{r} 88 \\ -\ 26 \\ \hline \end{array}$	**k.** $\begin{array}{r} 86 \\ -\ 14 \\ \hline \end{array}$	**q.** $\begin{array}{r} 36 \\ -\ 32 \\ \hline \end{array}$	**w.** $\begin{array}{r} 46 \\ -\ 41 \\ \hline \end{array}$
f. $\begin{array}{r} 61 \\ -\ 33 \\ \hline \end{array}$	**l.** $\begin{array}{r} 53 \\ -\ 32 \\ \hline \end{array}$	**r.** $\begin{array}{r} 97 \\ -\ 60 \\ \hline \end{array}$	**x.** $\begin{array}{r} 77 \\ -\ 63 \\ \hline \end{array}$

Word Problems

Read each word problem. Write the number sentence it describes. Find the difference.

a

Farmer Cole raised 93 bushels of wheat. Farmer Dale raised 68 bushels. What is the difference in the number of bushels each raised?

b

Dennis scored 43 points in his basketball game. Claire scored 40. What is the difference in points scored?

c

Jason bought a pair of shoes for 53 dollars. Clark bought a pair for 28 dollars. What is the difference paid?

d

Jill counted 83 ants near an ant hill. Jack counted 62. What is the difference in the ants counted?

Subtraction Solutions

Fill in the puzzle by solving the subtraction problems. Use the word names in the Word List.

Word List

eleven	thirteen	fifteen	seventeen	nineteen
twelve	fourteen	sixteen	eighteen	twenty

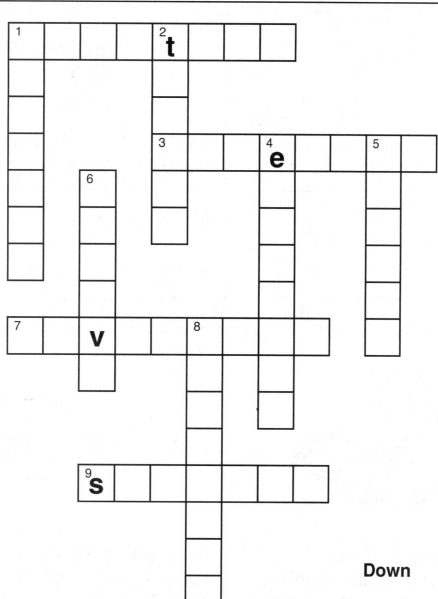

Across

1. 25 − 11 =
3. 40 − 21 =
7. 33 − 16 =
9. 51 − 35 =

Down

1. 46 − 31 =
2. 27 − 7 =
4. 22 − 4 =
5. 19 − 8 =
6. 44 − 32 =
8. 38 − 25 =

Using the Multiplication Chart

The multiplication chart shown here can be used to find any basic multiplication fact until you have learned them all.

One of the best ways to learn the facts is to practice using the chart.

	Columns											
	1	**2**	**3**	**4**	**5**	**6**	**7**	**8**	**9**	**10**	**11**	**12**
1	1	2	3	4	5	6	7	8	9	10	11	12
2	2	4	6	8	10	12	14	16	18	20	22	24
3	3	6	9	12	15	18	21	24	27	30	33	36
4	4	8	12	16	20	24	28	32	36	40	44	48
5	5	10	15	20	25	30	35	40	45	50	55	60
6	6	12	18	24	30	36	42	48	54	60	66	72
7	7	14	21	28	35	42	49	56	63	70	77	84
8	8	16	24	32	40	48	56	64	72	80	88	96
9	9	18	27	36	45	54	63	72	81	90	99	108
10	10	20	30	40	50	60	70	80	90	100	110	120
11	11	22	33	44	55	66	77	88	99	110	121	132
12	12	24	36	48	60	72	84	96	108	120	132	144

(Rows)

Read **down** for the **Columns**.

Read **across** for the **Rows**.

Note: To find 8 times 7, run one finger down the 8 column and a finger on the other hand across the 7 row until they meet. The answer is the number 56 where the row and column intersect (meet).

Directions: Use the chart to do these problems.

1.   5
   x 7

2.   7
   x 4

3.   4
   x 6

4.   9
   x 3

5.   7
   x 3

6.   5
   x 6

7.   9
   x 4

8.   4
   x 5

Multiplication Practice

Directions: Do these problems. Use your multiplication chart on page 110 if needed.

1.   8
   x 9

2.   7
   x 5

3.   5
   x 7

4.   11
   x 7

5.   11
   x 6

6.   4
   x 2

7.   8
   x 0

8.   6
   x 9

9.   8
   x 5

10.   0
   x 11

11.   5
   x 6

12.   7
   x 7

13.   5
   x 8

14.   7
   x 9

15.   4
   x 7

16.   4
   x 6

17.   3
   x 10

18.   5
   x 5

19.   7
   x 4

20. 12
   x 6

21. 9 x 11= _____

22. 6 x 11 = _____

23. 12 x 5 = _____

24. 8 x 12 = _____

25. 11 x 10 = _____

26. 6 x 9 = _____

27. 5 x 11 = _____

28. 7 x 12 = _____

29. 6 x 12 = _____

Multiplying with Three Factors

Directions: Compute the answer to each problem by multiplying two of the factors. Then multiply that product by the third factor. Use the multiplication chart on page 110 if needed. The first one has been done for you.

1. $3 \times 4 \times 5 =$
   $3 \times 4 = 12$
   $12 \times 5 = 60$

   Answer: __60__

2. $4 \times 2 \times 5 =$
   $4 \times 2 = 8$
   $8 \times 5 =$

   Answer: _____

3. $5 \times 6 \times 4 =$
   $5 \times 6 =$
   $30 \times 4 =$

   Answer: _____

4. $4 \times 6 \times 3 =$

   Answer: _____

5. $6 \times 5 \times 3 =$

   Answer: _____

6. $4 \times 9 \times 2 =$

   Answer: _____

7. $7 \times 4 \times 2 =$

   Answer: _____

8. $9 \times 8 \times 2 =$

   Answer: _____

9. $10 \times 5 \times 3 =$

   Answer: _____

10. $5 \times 3 \times 8 =$

    Answer: _____

11. $6 \times 10 \times 4 =$

    Answer: _____

12. $5 \times 8 \times 8 =$

    Answer: _____

13. $7 \times 8 \times 5 =$

    Answer: _____

14. $5 \times 7 \times 2 =$

    Answer: _____

15. $8 \times 6 \times 10 =$

    Answer: _____

Using One-Digit Multipliers with Two-and Three-Digit Multiplicands

Step by Step

1. Multiply 5 (ones) times 3 (ones) to equal 15 (1 ten and 5 ones).

2. Write the 5 below the line (in the ones place) and regroup by carrying 1 (ten) above the tens column.

3. Multiply 5 times 9 (tens) to equal 45 (tens).

4. Add the 1 (ten) that was carried over from the ones column to the 45 (tens). Write the 6 below the line (in the tens place) and regroup by carrying the 4 (hundreds) above the hundreds column.

5. Multiply 5 times 1 (hundred) to equal 5 (hundreds).

6. Add the regrouped 4 (hundreds) to the 5 (hundreds) to equal 9 hundreds.

7. The answer is 965.

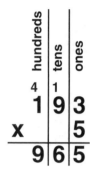

Directions: Use the example above as a guide to solve the following problems.

1. 42
   x 4

2. 51
   x 7

3. 44
   x 2

4. 12
   x 4

5. 48
   x 8

6. 63
   x 9

7. 48
   x 7

8. 35
   x 5

9. 65
   x 8

10. 34
    x 6

11. 98
    x 4

12. 76
    x 7

13. 133
    x 2

14. 233
    x 3

15. 623
    x 3

One-digit Multipliers and Two-digit Multiplicands (Regrouping)

Directions: Do these problems. Use your multiplication chart if needed. The first one has been done for you.

1.
```
  1
  43
x  6
 258
```

2.
```
 64
x 5
```

3.
```
 25
x 5
```

4.
```
 35
x 7
```

5.
```
 78
x 5
```

6.
```
 37
x 9
```

7.
```
 88
x 6
```

8.
```
 36
x 2
```

9.
```
 77
x 7
```

10.
```
 93
x 3
```

11.
```
 66
x 7
```

12.
```
 87
x 9
```

13.
```
 47
x 8
```

14.
```
 89
x 9
```

15.
```
 28
x 4
```

16.
```
 56
x 7
```

17. 33 x 7 = _____

18. 99 x 9 = _____

19. 65 x 7 = _____

20. 77 x 4 = _____

Using Two-Digit Multipliers with Three-Digit Multiplicands

Step by Step

1. Multiply 409 times 8 which equals 3,272.

2. Place an automatic zero (placeholder) in the ones place when multiplying 409 times 3 (tens) which equals 12,270.

3. Add the two partial products (3,272 + 12,270 = 15,542). Don't forget to add a comma every three digits starting from the ones place.

```
    409
  x  38
  3,272
+12,270
 15,542
```

Directions: Use the information above to help solve the problems on this page. The first one has been done for you.

1. 507
  x 37
  3,549
+15,210
 18,759

2. 609
  x 58

3. 706
  x 76

4. 108
  x 25

5. 607
  x 45

6. 304
  x 39

7. 107
  x 98

8. 509
  x 76

9. 608
  x 88

10. 706
  x 99

11. 405
  x 55

12. 407
  x 66

13. 231
  x 78

14. 289
  x 65

15. 578
  x 93

16. 374
  x 69

Multiplying by Multiples of 10 and Three-digit Multiplicands

Directions: Do these problems. Use your multiplication chart on page 110 if needed. The first one has been done for you.

1.
```
    1
  423
x  40
16,920
```

2.
```
  231
x  50
```

3.
```
  321
x  60
```

4.
```
  116
x  30
```

5.
```
  511
x  40
```

6.
```
  317
x  30
```

7.
```
  419
x  40
```

8.
```
  832
x  40
```

9.
```
  800
x  50
```

10.
```
  600
x  60
```

11.
```
  400
x  40
```

12.
```
  900
x  30
```

13.
```
  509
x  30
```

14.
```
  708
x  70
```

15.
```
  804
x  70
```

16.
```
  606
x  60
```

17.
```
  430
x  30
```

18.
```
  670
x  40
```

19.
```
  980
x  40
```

20.
```
  450
x  80
```

116

Two-digit Multiplicands (Regrouping)

Directions: Do these problems. Use your multiplication chart on page 110 if needed. The first one has been done for you.

```
        2
1.     53
     x 29
      477
   +1,060
    1,537
```

```
2.     59
     x 38
```

```
3.     68
     x 28
```

```
4.     19
     x 73
```

```
5.     63
     x 87
```

```
6.     69
     x 52
```

```
7.     29
     x 84
```

```
8.     93
     x 54
```

```
9.     33
     x 27
```

```
10.    57
     x 63
```

```
11.    66
     x 22
```

```
12.    17
     x 83
```

```
13.    30
     x 98
```

```
14.    80
     x 76
```

```
15.    60
     x 59
```

```
16.    20
     x 29
```

17. 45 x 93 = _____

18. 78 x 39 = _____

Multiplication Number Search

Directions: Find ten multiplication problems and answers hidden in the grid below. The problems can be hidden horizontally, vertically, or diagonally. When you are finished, make a blank grid to create your own multiplication number search. Challenge a friend to solve it!

7	9	8	2	16	5	1
8	5	4	20	3	7	15
56	45	32	43	9	6	11
21	9	50	8	9	5	3
7	3	21	12	81	30	2
6	9	54	7	6	42	2
18	27	20	39	4	8	16

118

Magical Multiplication

Directions: Multiply going across and down. Write the missing numbers. Study the example.

Example

X→		
5	5	25
6	2	12
30	10	300

Square #1

X→		
2		14
	5	
12		420

Square #2

X→		
10		20
	6	
40		480

Square #3

X→		
6		6
	3	
66		198

Multiplication: Found Ya!

Directions: In each grid below, circle the three numbers in a row that equal the number in the circle when multiplied. The numbers can be in a vertical, horizontal, or diagonal line.

48

1.

3	1	9
6	2	7
4	5	8

120

2.

8	6	4
9	5	2
7	1	3

180

3.

1	3	8
7	6	2
4	5	9

42

4.

7	3	2
1	4	8
9	6	5

100

5.

4	9	5
7	3	5
0	2	4

108

6.

2	7	5
9	9	9
6	3	8

24

7.

2	4	6
0	2	8
2	7	9

72

8.

7	8	2
6	4	3
9	4	1

162

9.

6	3	7
2	6	4
8	9	8

Multiplying the Minutes

Directions: Solve each word problem. Rewrite the time in hours and minutes.

1. Annette practices the piano every day for 20 minutes. How many minutes does Annette practice in one week?

_____ minutes or

_____ hours _____ minutes

2. Starla goes to gymnastics class 3 times a week for 45 minutes each time. How many minutes does Starla spend in gymnastics class in one week?

_____ minutes or

_____ hours _____ minutes

3. Nick has baseball practice 4 times a week. Each practice lasts 90 minutes. How many minutes each week does Nick have baseball practice?

_____ minutes or

_____ hours _____ minutes

4. Elisabeth sings twice a week for 50 minutes each time. How many minutes each week does Elisabeth sing?

_____ minutes or

_____ hours _____ minutes

5. Max jogs 4 times a week for 35 minutes each time. How many minutes does Max jog each week?

_____ minutes or

_____ hours _____ minutes

6. Harry lifts weights 4 times each week. He spends 30 minutes each time. How many minutes does Harry lift weights each week?

_____ minutes or

_____ hours _____ minutes

Using a Multiplication Chart for Division

The multiplication chart on page 110 can be used to find any basic division fact until you have learned them all.

To find the answer to 24 ÷ 8, you can run your finger down the 8 column until you reach 24. Then run your finger across the row until you find the row's original number.

Columns

		1	2	3	4	5	6	7	8
Rows	**1**	1	2	3	4	5	6	7	8
	2	2	4	6	8	10	12	14	16
	3	3	6	9	12	15	18	21	24

24 ÷ 8 = 3

Directions: Use the multiplication chart on page 110 if needed to solve the following problems.

1. $54 \div 6 =$

2. $49 \div 7 =$

3. $40 \div 8 =$

4. $36 \div 4 =$

5. $72 \div 9 =$

6. $56 \div 8 =$

7. $\dfrac{77}{11} =$

8. $\dfrac{45}{5} =$

9. $\dfrac{21}{3} =$

10. $\dfrac{99}{11} =$

11. $\dfrac{60}{12} =$

12. $\dfrac{28}{7} =$

13. $5\overline{)60}$

14. $6\overline{)72}$

15. $5\overline{)35}$

16. $3\overline{)33}$

17. $8\overline{)56}$

18. $10\overline{)90}$

19. $9\overline{)81}$

20. $4\overline{)36}$

21. $7\overline{)35}$

22. $4\overline{)16}$

23. $5\overline{)25}$

24. $6\overline{)36}$

25. $42 \div 6 =$

26. $42 \div 7 =$

27. $56 \div 8 =$

28. $56 \div 7 =$

Dividing Two Digits by One Digit

How would you solve the following problems?

$$6\overline{)43} \qquad 7\overline{)50}$$

For the first problem, you know that 6 x 7 = 42 is the nearest multiple of 6 to 43 so

$$\begin{array}{r} 7\text{ R1} \\ 6\overline{)43} \\ -42 \\ \hline 1 \end{array}$$

Remember: 6 x 7 = 42
42 + 1 = 43

For the second problem, you know that 7 x 7 = 49 is the nearest multiple of 7 to 50 so

$$\begin{array}{r} 7\text{ R1} \\ 7\overline{)50} \\ -49 \\ \hline 1 \end{array}$$

Remember: 7 x 7 = 49
49 + 1 = 50

Directions: Use the multiplication chart on page 110 to help you solve these problems.

1. $6\overline{)31}$ 2. $5\overline{)36}$ 3. $7\overline{)22}$ 4. $5\overline{)26}$

5. $6\overline{)19}$ 6. $4\overline{)25}$ 7. $9\overline{)82}$ 8. $5\overline{)41}$

9. $7\overline{)57}$ 10. $8\overline{)65}$ 11. $7\overline{)64}$ 12. $3\overline{)28}$

13. $7\overline{)31}$ 14. $8\overline{)35}$ 15. $6\overline{)39}$ 16. $5\overline{)29}$

17. $6\overline{)29}$ 18. $8\overline{)28}$ 19. $9\overline{)85}$ 20. $8\overline{)47}$

21. $6\overline{)57}$ 22. $8\overline{)55}$ 23. $9\overline{)69}$ 24. $8\overline{)38}$

Divisibility with 2 and 4

Reminders

- A dividend is evenly divisible by a divisor if it can be divided by that divisor with no remainder.
- Any number ending in 0, 2, 4, 6, or 8 is evenly divisible by 2.
- A number is evenly divisible by 4 if the last two digits are multiples of 4 such as 12, 16, 20, 24, 28, etc.

Directions: Do these problems. Use your multiplication chart on page 110 if you are unsure of your division facts. The first one is done for you.

1.
$$
\begin{array}{r}
91 \\
2\overline{)182} \\
-18 \\
\hline
2 \\
-2 \\
\hline
0
\end{array}
$$

2. $4\overline{)724}$

3. $2\overline{)628}$

4. $2\overline{)826}$

5. $4\overline{)928}$

6. $2\overline{)768}$

7. $2\overline{)518}$

8. $4\overline{)616}$

9. $2\overline{)924}$

10. $2\overline{)7,324}$

11. $4\overline{)8,744}$

12. $4\overline{)1,992}$

13. $2\overline{)2,826}$

14. $4\overline{)6,716}$

15. $4\overline{)8,984}$

16. $2\overline{)1,718}$

Dividing by Multiples of 10

There are 30 students in Mr. Park's class. There are 960 buttons in a jar. Mr. Park needs to distribute the buttons evenly for a class game. How many buttons can each student receive?

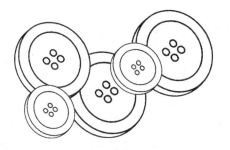

```
        x32
   30) 960
      - 90
        60
      - 60
         0
```

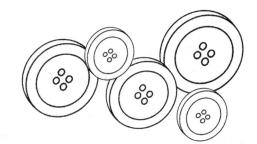

Each student can receive 32 buttons.

Directions: Solve the problems below.

1.
```
        x
   20) 680
```

2.
```
        x
   40) 840
```

3.
```
        x
   40) 880
```

4.
```
        x
   30) 870
```

5.
```
        x
   20) 480
```

6.
```
        x
   30) 690
```

7.
```
        x
   20) 840
```

8.
```
        x
   60) 660
```

9.
```
        x
   20) 420
```

10.
```
        x
   50) 550
```

11.
```
        x
   20) 640
```

12.
```
        x
   40) 640
```

Divisibility with 5, 10, and 100

Reminders

- A dividend is evenly divisible by a divisor if it can be divided by that divisor with no remainder.
- Any number ending in 0 or 5 is evenly divisible by 5.
- Any number ending in 0 is evenly divisible by 10.
- Any number ending in 00 is evenly divisible by 100.

Directions: Solve these problems. Use your multiplication chart on page 110 if you are unsure of your division facts. The first one is done for you.

1.
$$\begin{array}{r} 56 \\ 10\overline{)560} \\ -50 \\ \hline 60 \\ -60 \\ \hline 0 \end{array}$$

2. $10\overline{)880}$

3. $10\overline{)340}$

4. $5\overline{)450}$

5. $5\overline{)835}$

6. $5\overline{)645}$

7. $100\overline{)800}$

8. $100\overline{)500}$

9. $100\overline{)300}$

10. $10\overline{)5,660}$

11. $10\overline{)9,390}$

12. $10\overline{)300}$

13. $5\overline{)8,755}$

14. $5\overline{)7,070}$

15. $5\overline{)7,080}$

16. $100\overline{)4,600}$

Two-Digit Divisors/
Three-Digit Dividends

Directions: Solve these problems. Use your multiplication chart on page 110 if you are unsure of your division facts. The first one is done for you.

1.
$$\begin{array}{r} 4 \ \text{R}10 \\ 40\overline{)170} \\ -160 \\ \hline 10 \end{array}$$

2. $20\overline{)190}$

3. $60\overline{)150}$

4. $60\overline{)370}$

5. $50\overline{)230}$

6. $40\overline{)250}$

7. $70\overline{)220}$

8. $90\overline{)460}$

9. $40\overline{)390}$

10. $70\overline{)170}$

11. $60\overline{)290}$

12. $70\overline{)750}$

13. $30\overline{)260}$

14. $70\overline{)440}$

15. $20\overline{)550}$

16. $70\overline{)430}$

Dividing with Money

Directions: Solve these problems. Don't forget to use dollar signs and decimal points. Use your multiplication chart on page 110 if you are unsure of your division facts. The first one is done for you.

1.
$$
\begin{array}{r}
\$.99 \\
5\overline{)\$4.95} \\
-45 \\
\hline
45 \\
-45 \\
\hline
0
\end{array}
$$

2. $4\overline{)\$2.84}$

3. $9\overline{)\$6.39}$

4. $2\overline{)\$8.80}$

5. $9\overline{)\$3.24}$

6. $6\overline{)\$9.18}$

7. $8\overline{)\$9.60}$

8. $5\overline{)\$8.90}$

9. $4\overline{)\$2.36}$

10. $7\overline{)\$8.47}$

11. $9\overline{)\$9.36}$

12. $4\overline{)\$8.92}$

13. $5\overline{)\$88.35}$

14. $7\overline{)\$77.14}$

15. $9\overline{)\$88.11}$

16. $4\overline{)\$21.88}$

Divisibility with 20 and 25

Reminders

- A dividend is evenly divisible by a divisor if it can be divided by that divisor with no remainder.
- Any number ending in 00, 20, 40, 60, or 80 is evenly divisible by 20.
- Any number ending in 00, 25, 50, or 75 is evenly divisible by 25.

Directions: Do these problems. Use your multiplication chart on page 110 if you are unsure of your division facts. The first one has been done for you.

1.
$$
\begin{array}{r}
7 \\
25\overline{)175} \\
-175 \\
\hline
0
\end{array}
$$

2. $25\overline{)525}$

3. $25\overline{)425}$

4. $25\overline{)575}$

5. $25\overline{)925}$

6. $25\overline{)500}$

7. $20\overline{)400}$

8. $20\overline{)140}$

9. $20\overline{)180}$

10. $20\overline{)240}$

11. $20\overline{)880}$

12. $20\overline{)700}$

13. $25\overline{)3,125}$

14. $25\overline{)1,150}$

15. $25\overline{)8,875}$

16. $20\overline{)8,820}$

Division Number Search

Directions: Find ten division problems and answers hidden in the grid below. The problems may be hidden horizontally, vertically, or diagonally. When you are finished, use a blank grid to create your own division number search. Challenge a friend to solve it!

45	1	49	7	24	21	6
9	28	7	4	8	3	11
5	12	7	36	3	7	42
24	6	4	15	18	28	72
30	2	9	56	21	6	8
10	5	2	8	4	17	9
12	3	4	7	19	8	3

Dandy Division Squares

Directions: Divide going across and down. Write the missing numbers. Study the example.

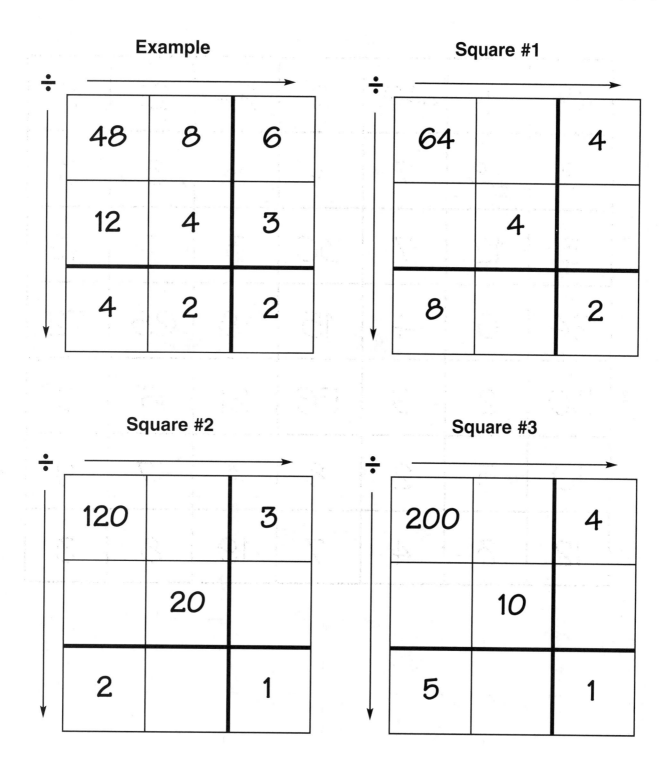

Mystery Message Division

Directions: The top boxes contain division problems, and the bottom boxes contain the answers. Work each problem and find its answer in the bottom boxes. Then, write the word from the problem box into the correct answer box. Your result will be a funny message.

Problems

$6\overline{)198}$	$4\overline{)5,627}$	$3\overline{)401}$	$8\overline{)1,032}$
who	**me**	**said**	**the**
$5\overline{)8,971}$	$7\overline{)368}$	$9\overline{)872}$	$2\overline{)3,074}$
in	**weeder**	**Martians**	**take**
$6\overline{)6,784}$	$4\overline{)819}$	$3\overline{)9,070}$	$5\overline{)617}$
your	**garden**	**to**	**landed**

Answers

96 r8	33	123 r2	1,794 r1
129	204 r3	133 r2	1,537
1,406 r3	3,023 r1	1,130 r4	52 r4

Math

Identifying Fractions

A **fraction** is a number that names part of a whole thing. The number at the top is the numerator. It tells how many parts of the whole are present. The number at the bottom is the denominator. It tells how many parts there are in all.

Examples

 $\frac{1}{2}$ (There are two parts in the circle. One part is gray. Therefore, the fraction is $\frac{1}{2}$.)

 $\frac{3}{4}$ (There are four parts in the square. Three parts are gray. The fraction is $\frac{3}{4}$.)

Directions: Write a fraction for each picture.

1. 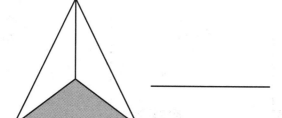 _____

2. 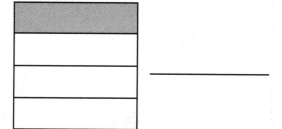 _____

3. 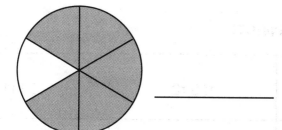 _____

4. 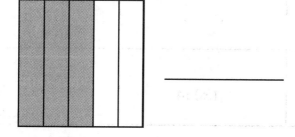 _____

5. 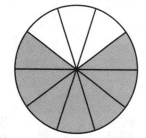 _____

6. 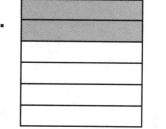 _____

7. 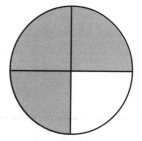 _____

8. 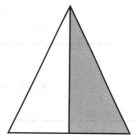 _____

Writing Fractions

A *fraction* is a part (or parts) of a whole item or shape.

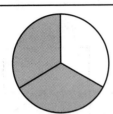 $\dfrac{2}{3}$

Two parts out of three are shaded.

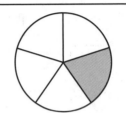 $\dfrac{1}{5}$

One part out of five is shaded.

Directions: Look at each shape. Write the fraction that tells how many parts of the whole object are shaded. The first one has already been done for you.

1.

$\dfrac{1}{3}$

2.

3.

4.

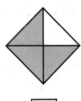

5.

6.

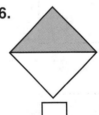

7.

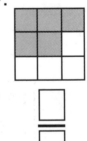

8.

9.

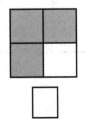

10.

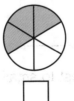

11.

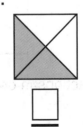

12.

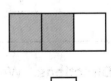

Ordering Fractions

Directions: Color in each circle to show the correct fraction.

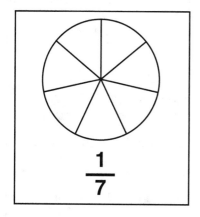

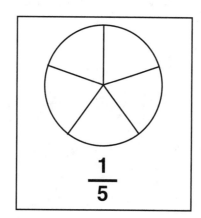

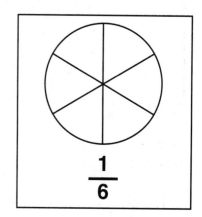

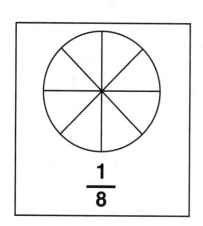

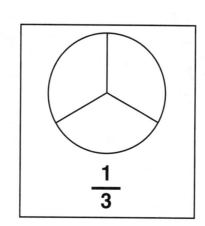

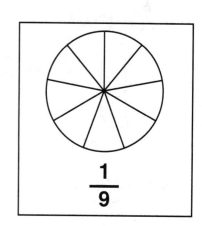

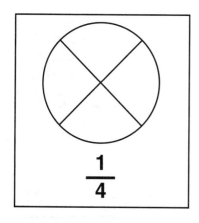

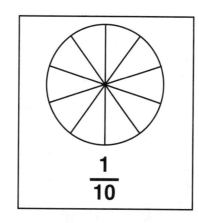

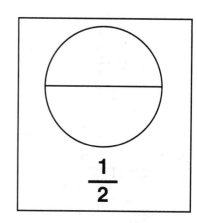

Directions: Write these fractions in order from largest to smallest.

_____, _____, _____, _____, _____, _____, _____, _____, _____

Math

Identifying Parts of a Whole and Parts of a Set

1. Write the fraction for one section.

2. Write the fraction for one section.

3. Write the fraction for one section.

4. Circle $\frac{1}{2}$ of the pictures. Write the answer.

$\frac{1}{2}$ of 10 = _____

5. Circle $\frac{1}{3}$ of the pictures. Write the answer.

$\frac{1}{3}$ of 9 = _____

6. Write the fraction for one section.

7. Write the fraction for one section.

8. Write the fraction for one section.

9. Divide the pictures into 3 equal sets. Complete the problem.

$\frac{2}{3}$ of 12 = _____

10. Divide the pictures into 6 equal sets. Complete the problem.

$\frac{3}{6}$ of 12 = _____

Naming Proper Fractions as Parts of a Whole

1. What fraction of the rectangle is *shaded*?

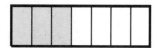

(A) $\frac{3}{7}$ (B) $\frac{3}{4}$ (C) $\frac{4}{7}$ (D) $\frac{1}{7}$

2. What fraction of the rectangle is *shaded*?

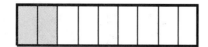

(A) $\frac{2}{9}$ (B) $\frac{2}{7}$ (C) $\frac{7}{9}$ (D) $\frac{1}{9}$

3. What fraction of the rectangle is *shaded*?

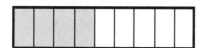

(A) $\frac{4}{9}$ (B) $\frac{1}{9}$ (C) $\frac{4}{5}$ (D) $\frac{5}{9}$

4. What fraction of the rectangle is *shaded*?

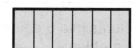

(A) $\frac{0}{6}$ (B) $\frac{6}{0}$ (C) $\frac{1}{6}$ (D) $\frac{6}{6}$

5. What fraction of the rectangle is *shaded*?

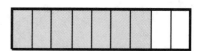

(A) $\frac{1}{9}$ (B) $\frac{7}{9}$ (C) $\frac{2}{9}$ (D) $\frac{7}{2}$

6. What fraction of the rectangle is *shaded*?

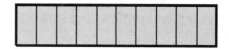

(A) $\frac{1}{10}$ (B) $\frac{10}{10}$ (C) $\frac{0}{10}$ (D) $\frac{10}{0}$

7. What fraction of the rectangle is *shaded*?

(A) $\frac{5}{7}$ (B) $\frac{1}{7}$ (C) $\frac{2}{7}$ (D) $\frac{5}{2}$

8. What fraction of the rectangle is *shaded*?

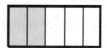

(A) $\frac{3}{5}$ (B) $\frac{1}{5}$ (C) $\frac{2}{3}$ (D) $\frac{2}{5}$

Identifying Equivalent Fractions

1. What equivalent fractions are *shaded*?

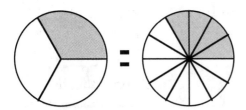

(A) $\dfrac{1}{3} = \dfrac{4}{8}$ (B) $\dfrac{5}{6} = \dfrac{1}{12}$

(C) $\dfrac{2}{3} = \dfrac{34}{360}$ (D) $\dfrac{1}{3} = \dfrac{4}{12}$

2. What equivalent fractions are *shaded*?

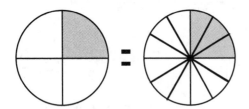

(A) $\dfrac{3}{4} = \dfrac{33}{360}$ (B) $\dfrac{1}{4} = \dfrac{3}{12}$

(C) $\dfrac{2}{3} = \dfrac{1}{12}$ (D) $\dfrac{1}{4} = \dfrac{3}{9}$

3. What equivalent fractions are *shaded*?

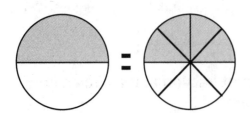

(A) $\dfrac{1}{2} = \dfrac{49}{360}$ (B) $\dfrac{1}{2} = \dfrac{4}{4}$

(C) $\dfrac{5}{4} = \dfrac{1}{8}$ (D) $\dfrac{1}{2} = \dfrac{4}{8}$

4. What equivalent fractions are *shaded*?

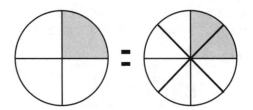

(A) $\dfrac{3}{4} = \dfrac{47}{360}$ (B) $\dfrac{3}{4} = \dfrac{1}{8}$

(C) $\dfrac{1}{4} = \dfrac{2}{8}$ (D) $\dfrac{1}{4} = \dfrac{2}{6}$

5. What equivalent fractions are *shaded*?

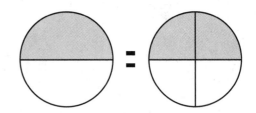

(A) $\dfrac{1}{2} = \dfrac{2}{2}$ (B) $\dfrac{1}{2} = \dfrac{2}{4}$

(C) $\dfrac{3}{2} = \dfrac{1}{4}$ (D) $\dfrac{1}{2} = \dfrac{92}{360}$

6. What equivalent fractions are *shaded*?

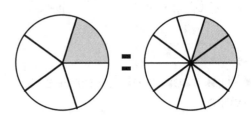

(A) $\dfrac{1}{5} = \dfrac{2}{8}$ (B) $\dfrac{4}{5} = \dfrac{38}{360}$

(C) $\dfrac{1}{5} = \dfrac{2}{10}$ (D) $\dfrac{3}{5} = \dfrac{1}{10}$

Naming Proper Fractions as Parts of a Set

1. What fraction of the circles is white?

(A) $\frac{4}{6}$ (B) $\frac{5}{2}$ (C) $\frac{2}{4}$ (D) $\frac{2}{6}$

2. What fraction of the circles is black?

(A) $\frac{5}{2}$ (B) $\frac{5}{7}$ (C) $\frac{2}{7}$ (D) $\frac{2}{5}$

3. What fraction of the circles is black?

(A) $\frac{3}{10}$ (B) $\frac{7}{10}$ (C) $\frac{7}{3}$ (D) $\frac{3}{7}$

4. What fraction of the circles is white?

(A) $\frac{1}{3}$ (B) $\frac{1}{2}$ (C) $\frac{5}{3}$ (D) $\frac{2}{3}$

5. What fraction of the circles is white?

(A) $\frac{6}{11}$ (B) $\frac{5}{6}$ (C) $\frac{5}{11}$ (D) $\frac{6}{5}$

6. What fraction of the circles is white?

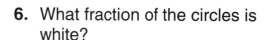

(A) $\frac{2}{6}$ (B) $\frac{4}{6}$ (C) $\frac{2}{4}$ (D) $\frac{5}{3}$

7. What fraction of the circles is black?

(A) $\frac{8}{3}$ (B) $\frac{8}{11}$ (C) $\frac{3}{8}$ (D) $\frac{3}{11}$

8. What fraction of the circles is black?

(A) $\frac{1}{6}$ (B) $\frac{5}{6}$ (C) $\frac{1}{5}$ (D) $\frac{5}{2}$

Adding Fractions with Like Denominators

Directions: Add the fractions and write the answer in simplest form.

1.

$$\frac{4}{7} + \frac{2}{7} = \underline{\quad}$$

2.

$$\frac{3}{5} + \frac{1}{5} = \underline{\quad}$$

3.

$$\frac{5}{12} + \frac{2}{12} = \underline{\quad}$$

4.

$$\begin{array}{r} \frac{6}{8} \\ \frac{1}{8} \\ + \underline{\quad} \end{array}$$

5.

$$\begin{array}{r} \frac{10}{18} \\ \frac{4}{18} \\ + \underline{\quad} \end{array}$$

6.

$$\frac{6}{14} + \frac{5}{14} = \underline{\quad}$$

7.

$$\begin{array}{r} \frac{8}{15} \\ \frac{1}{15} \\ + \underline{\quad} \end{array}$$

8.

$$\begin{array}{r} \frac{9}{17} \\ \frac{2}{17} \\ + \underline{\quad} \end{array}$$

9.

$$\begin{array}{r} \frac{4}{15} \\ \frac{1}{15} \\ + \underline{\quad} \end{array}$$

10.

$$\frac{6}{13} + \frac{1}{13} = \underline{\quad}$$

11.

$$\begin{array}{r} \frac{5}{8} \\ \frac{2}{8} \\ + \underline{\quad} \end{array}$$

12.

$$\begin{array}{r} \frac{12}{19} \\ \frac{3}{19} \\ + \underline{\quad} \end{array}$$

13.

$$\begin{array}{r} \frac{7}{20} \\ \frac{8}{20} \\ + \underline{\quad} \end{array}$$

14.

$$\frac{5}{16} + \frac{8}{16} = \underline{\quad}$$

15.

$$\begin{array}{r} \frac{4}{5} \\ \frac{1}{5} \\ + \underline{\quad} \end{array}$$

16.

$$\begin{array}{r} \frac{18}{30} \\ \frac{3}{30} \\ + \underline{\quad} \end{array}$$

Subtracting Fractions with Like Denominators

Directions: Subtract the fractions and write your answer in simplest form.

1.
$$\frac{4}{12}$$
$$-\frac{3}{12}$$

2.
$$\frac{7}{8}$$
$$-\frac{2}{8}$$

3.
$$\frac{13}{16}$$
$$-\frac{7}{16}$$

4.
$$\frac{3}{6}$$
$$-\frac{1}{6}$$

5.
$$\frac{5}{6}$$
$$-\frac{1}{6}$$

6.
$$\frac{2}{3}$$
$$-\frac{2}{3}$$

7.
$$\frac{9}{10}$$
$$-\frac{1}{10}$$

8.
$$\frac{7}{8}$$
$$-\frac{4}{8}$$

9.
$$\frac{3}{4}$$
$$-\frac{1}{4}$$

10.
$$\frac{2}{5}$$
$$-\frac{1}{5}$$

11.
$$\frac{10}{11}$$
$$-\frac{2}{11}$$

12.
$$\frac{9}{10}$$
$$-\frac{3}{10}$$

13.
$$\frac{9}{10}$$
$$-\frac{8}{10}$$

14.
$$\frac{11}{16}$$
$$-\frac{7}{16}$$

15.
$$\frac{7}{12}$$
$$-\frac{3}{12}$$

16.
$$\frac{13}{14}$$
$$-\frac{12}{14}$$

Adding and Subtracting Fractions

1. Subtract.

$$\frac{6}{8} - \frac{5}{8} =$$

2. Subtract.

$$\frac{4}{6} - \frac{3}{6} =$$

3. Add.

$$\frac{4}{7} + \frac{1}{7} =$$

4. Rewrite the answer as a mixed fraction.

$$\frac{2}{3} + \frac{2}{3} =$$

5. Rewrite the answer as a mixed fraction.

$$\frac{2}{4} + \frac{3}{4} =$$

6. Subtract.

$$\frac{6}{7} - \frac{3}{7} = \underline{\quad}$$

7. Subtract.

$$\frac{4}{8} - \frac{1}{8} = \underline{\quad}$$

8. Subtract.

$$\frac{2}{4} - \frac{1}{4} = \underline{\quad}$$

9. Solve.

The sugar bowl holds $\frac{3}{4}$ of a cup. Marnie used $\frac{1}{4}$ of a cup of sugar. How much sugar is left in the bowl?

There is _____ cup of sugar left.

10. Solve.

The container held $\frac{5}{6}$ of a cup of car wax. Harvey used $\frac{3}{6}$ of a cup to wax the car. How much wax is left?

There is _____ cup of wax left.

Writing Improper Fractions as Mixed Numbers

Directions: Rewrite these fractions as mixed numbers. Simplify where possible.

1. $\frac{5}{2} = $ _____

2. $\frac{4}{3} = $ _____

3. $\frac{13}{4} = $ _____

4. $\frac{12}{5} = $ _____

5. $\frac{7}{6} = $ _____

6. $\frac{10}{9} = $ _____

7. $\frac{9}{7} = $ _____

8. $\frac{8}{6} = $ _____

9. $\frac{10}{7} = $ _____

10. $\frac{8}{5} = $ _____

11. $\frac{9}{4} = $ _____

12. $\frac{3}{2} = $ _____

13. $\frac{5}{3} = $ _____

14. $\frac{15}{6} = $ _____

15. $\frac{14}{9} = $ _____

16. $\frac{8}{3} = $ _____

17. $\frac{7}{4} = $ _____

18. $\frac{11}{3} = $ _____

19. $\frac{12}{9} = $ _____

20. $\frac{17}{9} = $ _____

Mixed Practice with Fractions

In a **circle graph**, all the parts must add up to be a whole. Think of the parts like pieces that add up to one whole pie. Look at these pies and how they are divided into pieces.

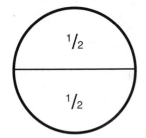

$\dfrac{1}{2}$ a pie

$+\ \dfrac{1}{2}$ a pie

2 halves =

1 whole pie

$\dfrac{1}{4}$ a pie

$+\ \dfrac{1}{4}$ a pie

$+\ \dfrac{1}{4}$ a pie

$+\ \dfrac{1}{4}$ a pie

4 fourths =

1 whole pie

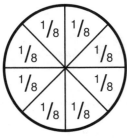

$\dfrac{1}{8}$ a pie

$+\ \dfrac{1}{8}$ a pie

$+\ \dfrac{1}{8}$ a pie

$+\ \dfrac{1}{8}$ a pie

$+\ \dfrac{1}{8}$ a pie

$+\ \dfrac{1}{8}$ a pie

$+\ \dfrac{1}{8}$ a pie

$+\ \dfrac{1}{8}$ a pie

8 eighths =

1 whole pie

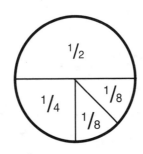

$\dfrac{1}{2}$ a pie = 1 half

$+\ \dfrac{1}{4}$ a pie = 1 fourth

$+\ \dfrac{1}{8}$ a pie = 1 eighth

$+\ \dfrac{1}{8}$ a pie = 1 eighth

1 whole pie

Make a circle graph to show how much pie a family ate. Here is the information you will need.

Mother ate $\dfrac{1}{4}$ of the pie.

Sister ate $\dfrac{1}{4}$ of the pie.

Father ate $\dfrac{1}{4}$ of the pie.

Brother ate $\dfrac{1}{8}$ of the pie.

Grandma ate $\dfrac{1}{8}$ of the pie.

Color the graph below using the Color

Pie My Family Ate

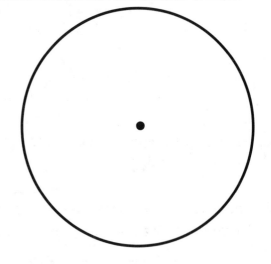

Color Key

sister = orange   mother = pink

grandma = red   brother = yellow

father = blue

Using Fractions

Three girls bought a chocolate cream pie. Joanna ate $\frac{1}{4}$ of the pie. Michelle ate $\frac{3}{8}$ of the pie. How much was left for Sara?

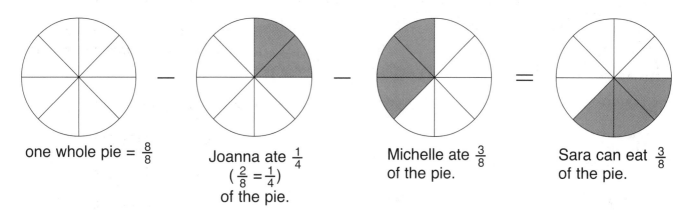

one whole pie = $\frac{8}{8}$

Joanna ate $\frac{1}{4}$
($\frac{2}{8} = \frac{1}{4}$)
of the pie.

Michelle ate $\frac{3}{8}$
of the pie.

Sara can eat $\frac{3}{8}$
of the pie.

Directions: Solve these fraction word problems.

1. Susan and Julie bought a ham and pineapple pizza. Susan ate $\frac{3}{7}$ of the pizza. How much was left for Julie? _____

2. Your best friend and you go to Pie Palace for pie. You eat $\frac{5}{6}$ of the pie. How much pie is left for your friend? _____

3. Your baseball coach bought a pizza to share with the team. The coach ate $\frac{7}{10}$ of the pizza. How much pizza was left for the team? _____

4. Your dad bought one whole vegetarian pizza from Pizza Palace. Your sister ate $\frac{5}{8}$ of the pizza before you got home. How much pizza was left for you? _____

5. James and Ralph bought a jalapeño pizza. James ate $\frac{2}{3}$ of the pizza. How much pizza was left for Ralph? _____

6. The third-grade teacher and the fourth-grade teacher bought a pepperoni pizza. The fourth-grade teacher ate $\frac{7}{12}$ of the pizza. How much pizza was left for the third-grade teacher? _____

7. The volleyball coach bought a sausage and olive pizza. He ate $\frac{3}{5}$ of the pizza. How much was left for his wife? _____

8. Your teacher and a friend bought a cheese pizza from Pizza Palace. Your teacher ate $\frac{1}{2}$ of the pizza. How much was left for the friend? _____

Funny Fraction

Directions: A funny message is hidden below. To find it, follow these directions. Find the fraction of the word in each problem below. As you find each fraction, write the letters in order on the lines at the bottom of the page. The first one has been done for you.

1. the first $\frac{1}{3}$ of ice

2. the first $\frac{2}{5}$ of water

3. the last $\frac{2}{5}$ of plant

4. the last $\frac{2}{3}$ of bed

5. the first $\frac{2}{4}$ of toad

6. the last $\frac{3}{4}$ of gown

7. the first $\frac{1}{2}$ of at

8. the first $\frac{2}{3}$ of bat

9. the first $\frac{2}{3}$ of key

10. the last $\frac{2}{4}$ of very

11. the first $\frac{3}{6}$ of butter

12. the last $\frac{1}{3}$ of ski

13. the first $\frac{3}{5}$ of count

14. the last $\frac{2}{4}$ of cold

15. the last $\frac{2}{4}$ of rant

16. the first $\frac{4}{6}$ of raisin

17. the last $\frac{1}{2}$ of me

18. the first $\frac{3}{4}$ of them

19. the first $\frac{2}{3}$ of dog

20. the last $\frac{3}{5}$ of cough

I ___ ___ ___ ___ ___ ___ ___ ___ ___ ___ ___ ___ ___

___ ___ ___ ___ ___ ___ ___ ___ ___ ___ ___

___ ___ ___ ___ ___ ___ ___ ___ ___ ___ ___

___ ___ ___ ___ ___ ___ ___ ___ ___ .

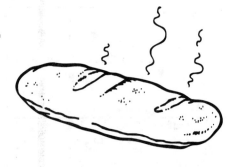

Adding Fractions Mystery Message

Directions: The top boxes contain fraction addition problems, and the bottom boxes contain the answers. Work each problem and find its answer in the bottom boxes. Then, write the word from the problem box into the correct answer box. Your result will be the answer to the question.

$\frac{1}{7}$ $+ \frac{5}{7}$ **crack**	$\frac{2}{4}$ $+ \frac{1}{4}$ **will**	$\frac{1}{2}$ $+ \frac{1}{2}$ **that**	$\frac{1}{5}$ $+ \frac{2}{5}$ **more**
$\frac{1}{6}$ $+ \frac{4}{6}$ **aster**	$\frac{2}{7}$ $+ \frac{1}{7}$	$\frac{3}{8}$ $+ \frac{2}{8}$	$\frac{2}{5}$ $+ \frac{2}{5}$
$\frac{1}{6}$ $+ \frac{2}{6}$ **and**	$\frac{3}{8}$ $+ \frac{4}{8}$ **have**	$\frac{1}{8}$ $+ \frac{1}{8}$ **I**	$\frac{1}{3}$ $+ \frac{1}{3}$ **like**

What did the painter say to the wall?

$\frac{3}{7}$	$\frac{3}{5}$	$\frac{6}{7}$	$\frac{2}{3}$
1	$\frac{3}{6}$ or $\frac{1}{2}$	$\frac{2}{8}$ or $\frac{1}{4}$	$\frac{3}{4}$
$\frac{7}{8}$	$\frac{5}{8}$	$\frac{4}{5}$	$\frac{5}{6}$

Plane Shapes and Solid Shapes

A **plane** shape is a shape that is flat and two dimensional. A **solid** shape is three dimensional. It has sides and a top and bottom.

Directions: Match each plane shape to its solid form.

1.

square

triangle

circle

rectangle

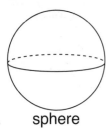
sphere

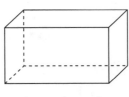
rectangular prism

triangular pyramid

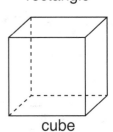
cube

Directions: Look at each solid shape. What plane figures do you see on its flat surfaces? Outline the plane figures. Write the name(s) of the plane figure(s) on the line(s).

2. rectangular prism

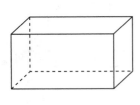

_____

and _____

3. rectangular pyramid

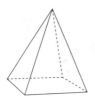

_____

and _____

4. cube

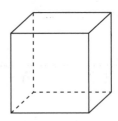

_____

5. cylinder

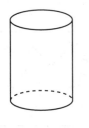

_____

6. cone

_____

7. triangular pyramid

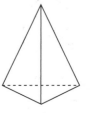

_____

Polygons

Polygons (*poly* = many, *gons* = angles) are shapes with many angles.

penta = five	hepta = seven	nona = nine
hexa = six	octa = eight	deca = ten

Directions: An angle is formed where two sides meet. Count the number of angles. Write the complete name of each shape on the line.

1.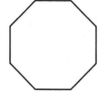

_____

2.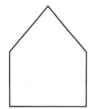

_____

3.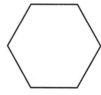

_____

4.

_____

5.

_____

6.

_____

Directions: Now try to classify these unusual shapes!

7.

_____

8.

_____

9.

_____

Parts of a Solid

Solids have three parts.

- **Face:** the flat surfaces
- **Edge:** where two faces meet
- **Vertex:** corner where three or more edges meet
- **Curved:** the surface is rounded, not flat

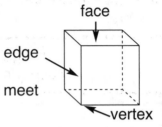
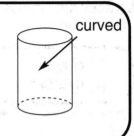

face

edge

vertex

curved

Directions: Count the number of flat surfaces, curved surfaces, edges, and vertices on each solid.

1.

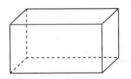

flat surfaces: _____

curved surfaces: _____

edges: _____

vertices: _____

2.

flat surfaces: _____

curved surfaces: _____

edges: _____

vertices: _____

3.

flat surfaces: _____

curved surfaces: _____

edges: _____

vertices: _____

4.

flat surfaces: _____

curved surfaces: _____

edges: _____

vertices: _____

5.

flat surfaces: _____

curved surfaces: _____

edges: _____

vertices: _____

6.

flat surfaces: _____

curved surfaces: _____

edges: _____

vertices: _____

7.

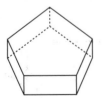

flat surfaces: _____

curved surfaces: _____

edges: _____

vertices: _____

8.

flat surfaces: _____

curved surfaces: _____

edges: _____

vertices: _____

9.

flat surfaces: _____

curved surfaces: _____

edges: _____

vertices: _____

Solid Patterns

Directions: Which solid figure would each pattern make?

cone	rectangular prism	rectangular pyramid
cylinder	cube	triangular pyramid

1.

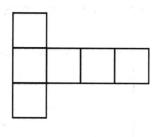

_____

2.

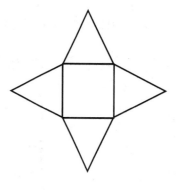

_____

3.

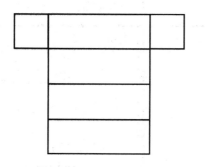

_____

4.

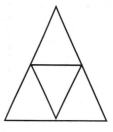

_____

5.

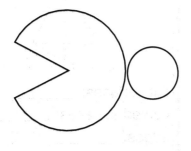

_____

6.

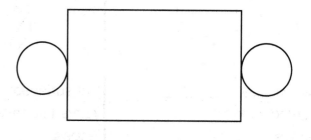

_____

Lines of Symmetry

Directions: A shape is symmetrical if, when folded in half, both parts overlap exactly. Look at the shapes below. Are they symmetrical?

1.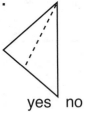

yes   no

2.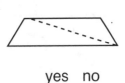

yes   no

3.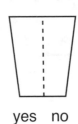

yes   no

4.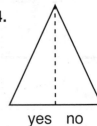

yes   no

5.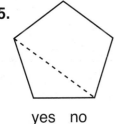

yes   no

6.

yes   no

7.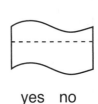

yes   no

8.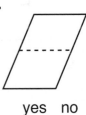

yes   no

Directions: Draw a line of symmetry for each shape.

9.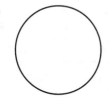

10.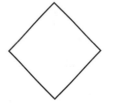

11.

12.

13.

14.

15.

16.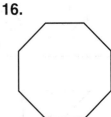

17.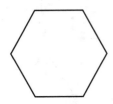

18.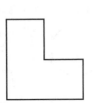

19.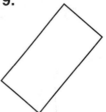

20.

More Than One Line of Symmetry

Directions: Circle the shape or shapes in each row that has more than one line of symmetry.

1.

2.

3.

4.

5.

6.

7.

Similar or Congruent?

Directions: Are the shapes similar or congruent? (Remember, congruent means "the same size and the same shape.") Circle the correct word.

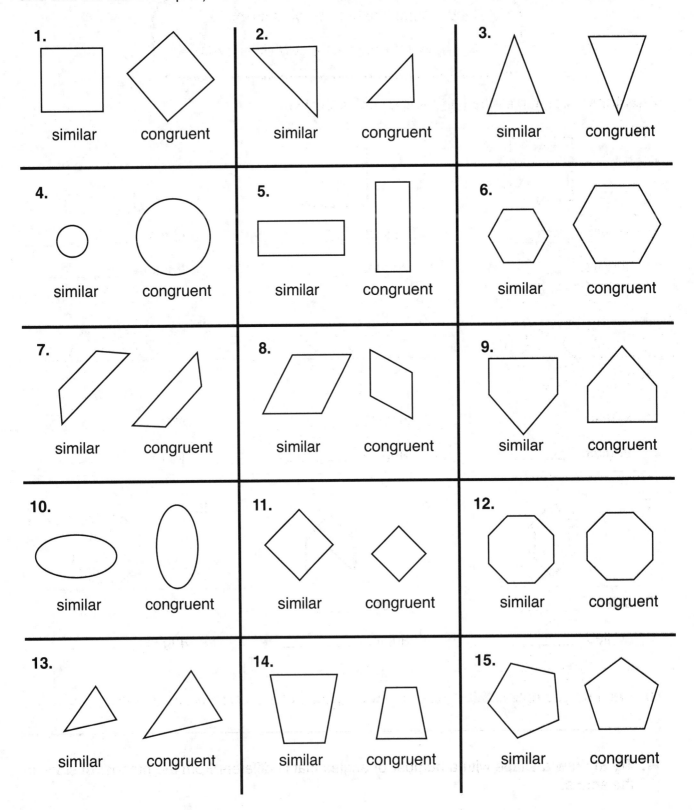

1. similar   congruent

2. similar   congruent

3. similar   congruent

4. similar   congruent

5. similar   congruent

6. similar   congruent

7. similar   congruent

8. similar   congruent

9. similar   congruent

10. similar   congruent

11. similar   congruent

12. similar   congruent

13. similar   congruent

14. similar   congruent

15. similar   congruent

Count Those Sides and Angles!

A **side** is the straight part on a shape.

An **angle** is formed when two sides meet.

Directions: Count the sides and angles on each shape.

1.

sides: _____

angles: _____

2.

sides: _____

angles: _____

3.

sides: _____

angles: _____

4.

sides: _____

angles: _____

5.

sides: _____

angles: _____

6.

sides: _____

angles: _____

7.

sides: _____

angles: _____

8.

sides: _____

angles: _____

9.

sides: _____

angles: _____

10. What do you notice about the number of sides and angles on each shape? _____

_____

11. Try to draw a shape with a number of angles that is different from the number of sides in the shape.

What Is an Angle?

An **angle** is formed when two lines meet.
The pennant has three angles.

The pencil has five angles.

 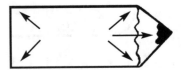

1. Circle the shapes below that have angles.

There are three different kinds of angles—acute angles, right angles, and obtuse angles.

Acute angles are less than 90°.
Acute angles do not make a square corner.

Right angles are exactly 90°.
Right angles make a square corner.

Obtuse angles are greater than 90°.
Obtuse angles do not make a square corner.

Directions: Identify angle *A* below. Is it an acute angle, a right angle, or an obtuse angle?

2.

_____

3.

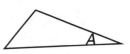

_____

4.

_____

5.

_____

6.

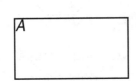

_____

7.

_____

Naming Angles

Directions: Look at the angle marked with an *. What kind of angle is it? Circle the correct answer.

1.

acute angle
right angle
obtuse angle

2.

acute angle
right angle
obtuse angle

3.

acute angle
right angle
obtuse angle

4.

acute angle
right angle
obtuse angle

5.

acute angle
right angle
obtuse angle

6.

acute angle
right angle
obtuse angle

7.

acute angle
right angle
obtuse angle

8.

acute angle
right angle
obtuse angle

9.

acute angle
right angle
obtuse angle

10.

acute angle
right angle
obtuse angle

11.

acute angle
right angle
obtuse angle

12.

acute angle
right angle
obtuse angle

Triangles: By the Sides

Triangles can be described by the number of **congruent** sides. **Congruent** means the sides are exactly the same.

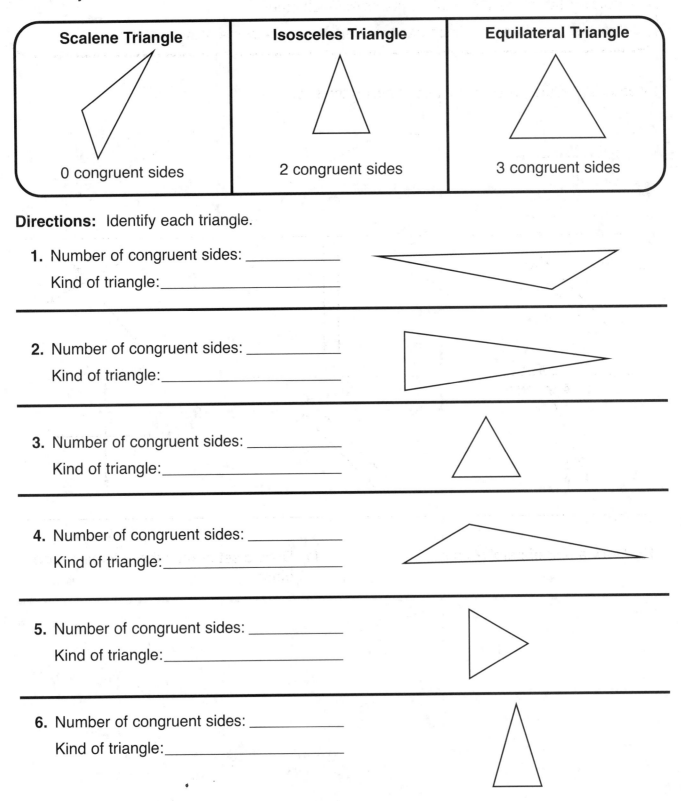

Scalene Triangle	Isosceles Triangle	Equilateral Triangle
0 congruent sides	2 congruent sides	3 congruent sides

Directions: Identify each triangle.

1. Number of congruent sides: _____

   Kind of triangle: _____

2. Number of congruent sides: _____

   Kind of triangle: _____

3. Number of congruent sides: _____

   Kind of triangle: _____

4. Number of congruent sides: _____

   Kind of triangle: _____

5. Number of congruent sides: _____

   Kind of triangle: _____

6. Number of congruent sides: _____

   Kind of triangle: _____

Parallel Lines and Intersecting Lines

- **Parallel lines** are lines that do not cross each other.
- **Intersecting lines** are lines that cross each other at some point.

Directions: Write *parallel* or *intersecting* on the line.

1.

_____

2.

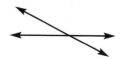

_____

3.

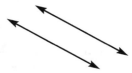

_____

4.

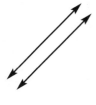

_____

5.

_____

6.

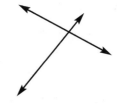

_____

7.

_____

8.

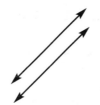

_____

9.

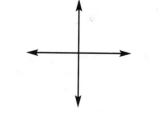

_____

10. Draw a pair of parallel lines.

11. Draw a set of lines that intersect each other.

 #3943 Mastering Fourth Grade Skills

More Work with Parallel and Intersecting Lines

Directions: Answer the questions about each set of lines.

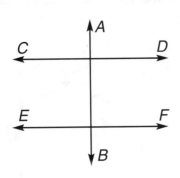

1. $\overleftrightarrow{CD}$ is parallel to which line? _____

2. $\overleftrightarrow{EF}$ is not parallel to which line? _____

3. $\overleftrightarrow{EF}$ is crossed by which line? _____

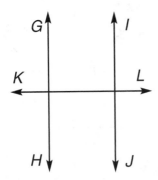

4. $\overleftrightarrow{GH}$ is parallel to which line? _____

5. Name a line that intersects $\overleftrightarrow{KL}$. _____

6. $\overleftrightarrow{IJ}$ is not parallel to which line? _____

Directions: Draw the following lines.

7. Draw $\overleftrightarrow{MN}$ parallel to $\overleftrightarrow{OP}$.

8. Draw $\overleftrightarrow{QR}$ intersecting $\overleftrightarrow{ST}$.

9. Draw $\overleftrightarrow{UV}$ parallel to $\overleftrightarrow{WX}$.

 Draw $\overleftrightarrow{YZ}$ intersecting $\overleftrightarrow{UV}$ and $\overleftrightarrow{WX}$.

10. Draw $\overleftrightarrow{AB}$ intersecting $\overleftrightarrow{CD}$.

 Draw $\overleftrightarrow{EF}$ parallel to $\overleftrightarrow{CD}$.

Perimeter

- Perimeter is the distance around a figure.
- To compute the perimeter of a rectangle, add two adjoining sides and multiply the sum by 2.
- Perimeter = (length + width) x 2
- $P = (l + w) \times 2$

6 cm

2 cm

P = (6 cm + 2 cm) x 2
P = 16 cm

Directions: Compute the perimeter of each rectangle.

1.

5 cm

4 cm

P = _____

2.

8 cm

3 cm

P = _____

3.

4 in.

3 in.

P = _____

4.

9 in.

5 in.

P = _____

5.

12 mm

9 mm

P = _____

6.

18 mm

10 mm

P = _____

7.

7 cm

4 cm

P = _____

8.

13 cm

6 cm

P = _____

9.

8 in.

6 in.

P = _____

Perimeter *(cont.)*

Directions: The **perimeter** *(P)* is the area around the outside of the shape. To find the perimeter, add all of the sides of the shape together.

1.

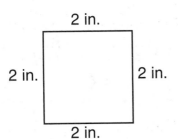

P = _____ in.

2.

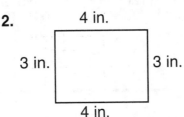

P = _____ in.

3.

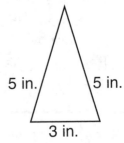

P = _____ in.

4.

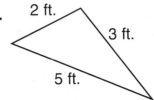

P = _____ ft.

5.

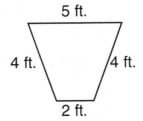

P = _____ ft.

6.

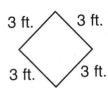

P = _____ ft.

7.

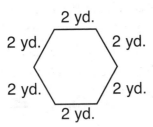

P = _____ yd.

8.

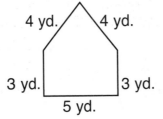

P = _____ yd.

9.

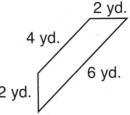

P = _____ yd.

10.

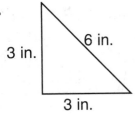

P = _____ in.

11.

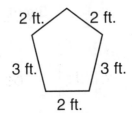

P = _____ ft.

12.

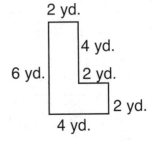

P = _____ yd.

The Right Amount of Space

To find the area of a square or rectangle multiply the length by the width.

Formula: Area = length x width = square units   A = l x w = sq. units

Directions: Find the correct amount of area for each animal. Write the letter on the line.

Legend

□ = 1 foot

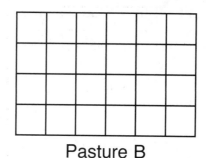

Pasture B

Pasture C

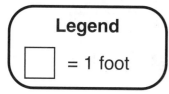

Pasture A

Pasture D

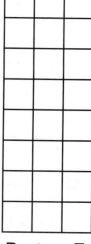

Pasture E

---

1. Gertie Giraffe needs at least 20 square feet. Which pastures would be a good fit for Gertie?

Pastures _____

and _____

2. Harry Hamster likes a nice, cozy space. Any pasture with less than 5 square feet would be a good fit for Harry. Which pasture would Harry like the best?

Pasture _____

3. Roberta Rattlesnake likes to slither in a space that has more than 6 square feet but less than 24 square feet. Which pasture would be a good fit for Roberta?

Pasture _____

4. Larry Ladybug likes a pasture that has one square foot for each one of his legs. Which pasture would be a good fit for Larry Ladybug?

Pasture _____

Finding the Areas of Squares and Rectangles

To find the area of a square or rectangle, multiply the length by the width.

Formula: Area = length x width = square units $A = l \times w =$ sq. units

Directions: Find the area for each square and rectangle.

1.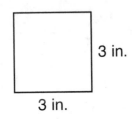

3 in.

3 in.

____ x ____ = ____ sq. in.

2.

7 in.

1 in.

____ x ____ = ____ sq. in.

3.

5 in.

5 in.

____ x ____ = ____ sq. in.

4.

3 in.

4 in.

____ x ____ = ____ sq. in.

5.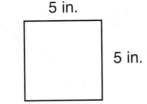

3 ft.

1 ft.

____ x ____ = ____ sq. ft.

6.

7 ft.

7 ft.

____ x ____ = ____ sq. ft.

7. What are the dimensions of a square with an area of 36 square inches? _____

8. What are the dimensions of a rectangle with an area of 40 square inches? _____

9. Would a square or a rectangle have an area of 50 square inches? _____

What would its measurements be? _____ x _____

Area of a Triangle

To find the area of a triangle, multiply the base *(b)* by the height *(h)* and divide by 2.

Formula: Area = $\underline{\text{base x height}}$ = square units $A = \underline{b \times h}$ = sq. units
          2   2

Directions: Find the area for each triangle.

1.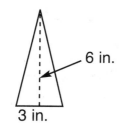

   _____ sq. in.

2.

   _____ sq. in.

3.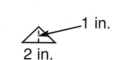

   _____ sq. in.

4.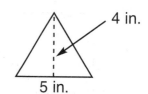

   _____ sq. in.

5.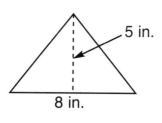

   _____ sq. in.

6.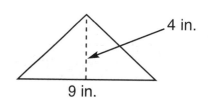

   _____ sq. in.

7. Make a triangle with an area of 12 sq. in.   **8.** Make a triangle with an area of 15 sq. in.

Volume of a Cube or a Rectangular Prism

Formula for a Cube	**Formula for a Rectangular Prism**
Volume = side x side x side = cubic units	Volume = length x width x height = cubic units
$V = s^3$ = cu. units	$V = l$ x w x h = cu. units

Directions: Measure each cube or rectangle to the nearest centimeter. Find the volume for each solid.

1.

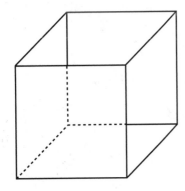

$s =$ _____ cm

_____ x _____ x _____ = _____ cu. cm

2.

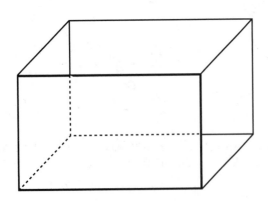

$l =$ _____ cm $w =$ _____ cm $h =$ _____ cm

_____ x _____ x _____ = _____ cu. cm

3.

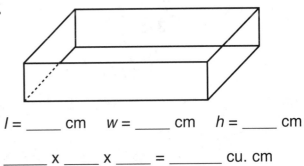

$l =$ _____ cm $w =$ _____ cm $h =$ _____ cm

_____ x _____ x _____ = _____ cu. cm

4.

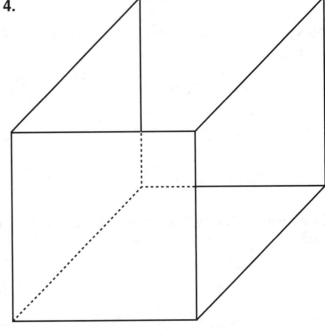

$s =$ _____ cm

_____ x _____ x _____ = _____ cu. cm

Circles

- **Center:** middle of the circle
- **Radius:** distance from the center of the circle to any point on the side of the circle
- **Diameter:** distance from one side of the circle to the opposite side going through the center
- **Circumference:** distance around the circle

Directions: Name the part of the circle to which the arrow is pointing.

1.

_____

2.

_____

3.

_____

4.

_____

5.

_____

6.

_____

Directions: The diameter *(d)* is twice the length of the radius *(r)*. What is the diameter of each circle?

7.

$d =$ _____ in.

8.

$d =$ _____ in.

9.

$d =$ _____ in.

Directions: The radius *(r)* is half the length of the diameter *(d)*. What is the radius of each circle?

10.

$r =$ _____ in.

11.

$r =$ _____ in.

12.

$r =$ _____ in.

Flips and Slides

Directions: A **flip** is when a picture is turned over. A **slide** is when the picture is moved over. Look at each pair of pictures. To go from the first picture to the second picture, was it flipped or did it slide? Circle the answer.

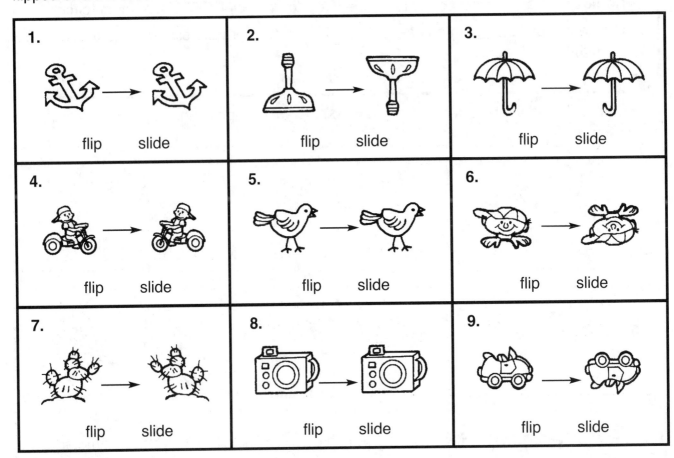

1. flip   slide

2. flip   slide

3. flip   slide

4. flip   slide

5. flip   slide

6. flip   slide

7. flip   slide

8. flip   slide

9. flip   slide

Directions: What comes next in each pattern?

10.

11.

12.

13.

Twists and Turns

An object can be rotated **clockwise** by degrees (or in other words—turned!).

Start   90° $\frac{1}{4}$ turn   180° $\frac{1}{2}$ turn   270° $\frac{3}{4}$ turn   360° full turn

Directions: To what degree was each item turned? Circle the answer.

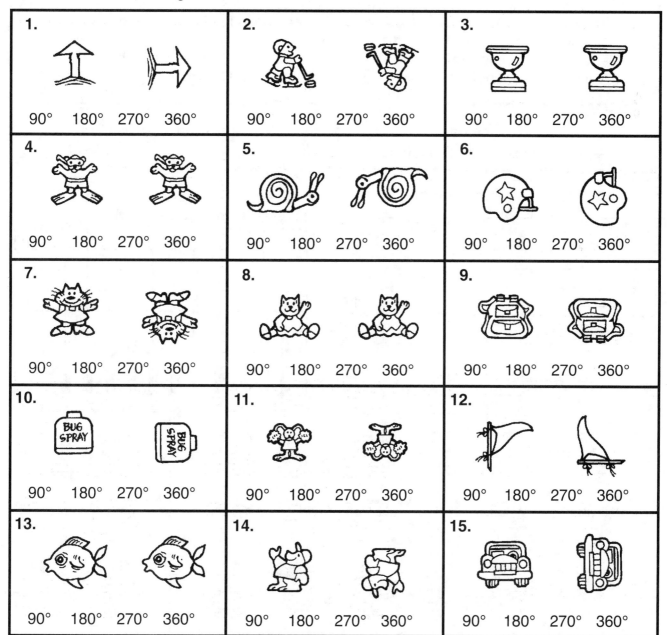

1. 90°   180°   270°   360°

2. 90°   180°   270°   360°

3. 90°   180°   270°   360°

4. 90°   180°   270°   360°

5. 90°   180°   270°   360°

6. 90°   180°   270°   360°

7. 90°   180°   270°   360°

8. 90°   180°   270°   360°

9. 90°   180°   270°   360°

10. 90°   180°   270°   360°

11. 90°   180°   270°   360°

12. 90°   180°   270°   360°

13. 90°   180°   270°   360°

14. 90°   180°   270°   360°

15. 90°   180°   270°   360°

What Are Charts, Graphs, and Diagrams?

Charts, graphs, and **diagrams** are visual tools. They give us a way to see information easily. It is sometimes easier to see information in a chart, graph, or diagram than to *hear* it or *read* it.

Read these results of a survey taken in a second grade class of 30 students. They were asked the month of their birth.

Three were born in January, five in February, and none in March. April had four student birthdays, and May had seven. There were two birthdays in both June and July, and three in August. September had two, and both October and November had one. There were no class birthdays in December.

Now, look at the same information presented in a chart, graph, and diagram. Is it easier for you to understand when you can see it?

Chart of Class Birthdays

Month	Number of Birthdays
January	3
February	5
March	0
April	4
May	7
June	2
July	2
August	3
September	2
October	1
November	1
December	0

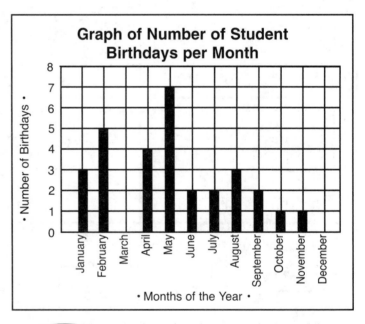

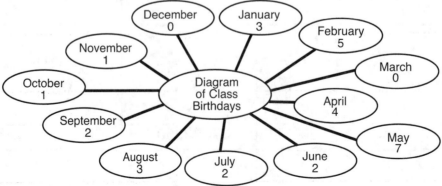

Tally Charts

We can keep a record of how many things we count on a piece of paper. An easy way to do this is to make a *tally chart.*

For every thing you count, you make a mark like this: |

How many marks are there? _____

To make it easier and faster to read, every fifth mark is crossed over the four marks that come before it like this: ||||

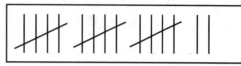

How many marks are there? _____

It is easier to count by fives than it is to count by ones on a tally chart.

> Read these tally charts. Write how many marks each tally has.

1.

2.

3.

4.

5.

6.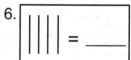

> Make tally charts for the numbers in the boxes below.

7. | = 5

8. | = 10

9. | =7

10. | = 13

11. | = 9

12. | = 17

Pictographs

One type of graph that gives us information is called a *pictograph*. In a pictograph, pictures are used instead of numbers.

Here is a pictograph that shows the number of fish caught each day at Canyon Lake.

Daily Fish Catch at Canyon Lake

Sunday	🐟 🐟 🐟 🐟 🐟 🐟 🐟
Monday	🐟 🐟
Tuesday	🐟
Wednesday	🐟 🐟 🐟
Thursday	🐟 🐟
Friday	🐟 🐟 🐟 🐟
Saturday	🐟 🐟 🐟 🐟 🐟

KEY: 🐟 = 10 fish

1. On what day were the most fish caught? _____

   How many fish were caught on this day? _____

2. On what day were 40 fish caught? _____

3. On what day were the fewest fish caught? _____

4. Were the same number of fish caught on Monday and Thursday? _____

   How many? _____

5. How many fish were caught on both Saturday and Sunday? _____

   (Add the two days together to get the total fish caught.)

Pictographs *(cont.)*

Read this pictograph to find out the amount and types of instruments sold in April at Harmony Music Store.

April Instrument Sales at Harmony Music Store	
pianos	
flutes	
guitars	
drums	
trumpets	

Key: 1 instrument = 5 instruments

1. How many of each of these instruments were sold?

   pianos _____ flutes _____ guitars _____

   drums_____trumpets _____

2. How many more guitars were sold than:

   pianos _____ flutes _____ drums _____ trumpets _____

3. Do you think the piano sales or the guitar sales brought in more money for Harmony Music Store? Explain the reason(s) for your choice.

   _____

   _____

Circle Graphs

One type of graph that gives us information is called a *circle graph*. In a circle graph, you can show how things are divided into the parts of a whole.

Shown in this circle graph are the types and amounts of fruit sold at a produce stand in a week in July.

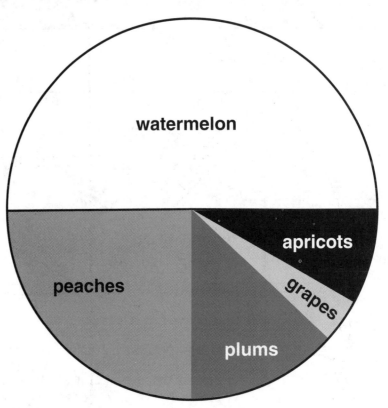

1. What fruit sold the most at O'Henry's Fruit Stand? _____

2. What fruit sold the least? _____

3. Rank the order of the fruits that were sold. Number 1 will be the fruit that sold most, number 5, least.

   1. _____   2. _____   3. _____

   4. _____   5. _____

4. Circle the correct fraction.

   Watermelon was $\frac{1}{2}$ $\frac{1}{4}$ $\frac{1}{3}$ of all the fruit sold.

   Peaches were $\frac{1}{4}$ $\frac{1}{2}$ $\frac{1}{5}$ of all the fruit sold.

   Plums were $\frac{1}{2}$ $\frac{1}{22}$ $\frac{1}{8}$ of all the fruit sold.

5. Which of the fruits represented on the circle graph is your

Under the Big Top

The circus has come to your town and you want to know as much as you can about the kinds of animals that are under the circus tent. You count them and record what you find out on a circle graph.

Kinds of Animals Under the Big Top

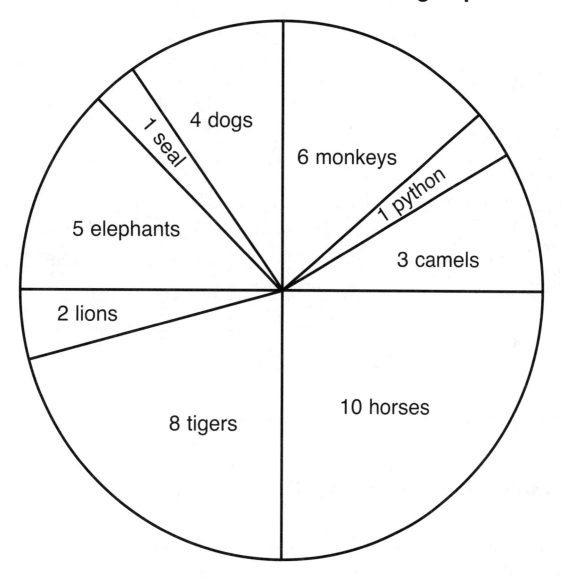

1. How many animals are under the "Big Top"? _____

2. Are there more tigers or monkeys? _____

3. What animals are the only ones of their kind? _____

4. What animal do you find most at the circus? _____

5. What animals in this circus might you see in your neighborhood? _____

Slices

In a circle graph, all the parts must add up to be a whole. Think of the parts as pieces that add up to one whole pie.

Look at this circle graph that shows what Chris did during one hour of time at home.

What Chris did from 4 P.M. to 5 P.M. on November 5.

1. How many minutes did Chris spend:

   doing homework? _____

   eating a snack? _____

   changing clothes? _____

   playing a video game? _____

   walking the dog? _____

2. How did you figure out the number of minutes?

   _____

   _____

Make a circle graph that shows what you did during one of your afterschool hours.

Write the title of your graph here.

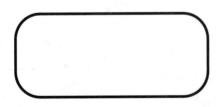

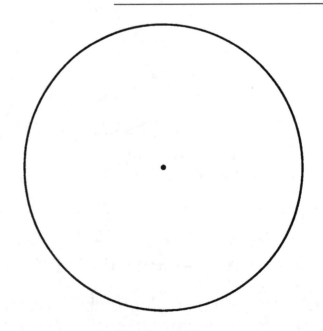

Bar Graphs

One type of graph that gives us information is called a *bar graph*. A bar graph shows us many different types of things by the height or length of the bars.

A **single bar graph** is one type of bar graph. Questions that ask what kind, what place, how much, how long, and how many can be answered by using a single bar graph.

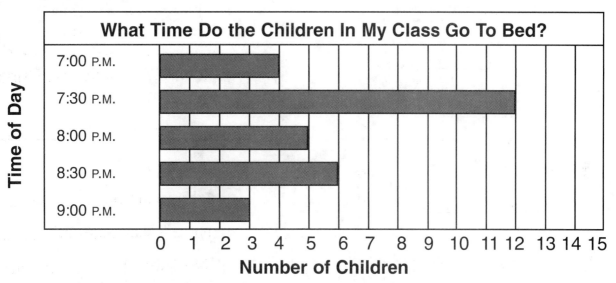

A **double bar graph** (or **multiple bar graph**) is another type of bar graph. It is used to compare two or more things.

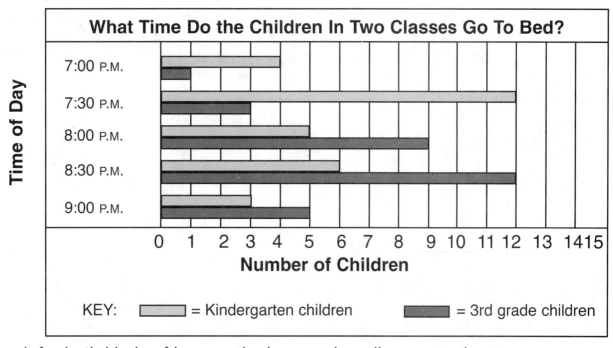

• Look for both kinds of bar graphs in encyclopedias, magazines, newspapers, or other resources. Share what you find with your class.

Which Class?

The classes at Barnsdale Elementary School kept a bar graph of the number of books each grade read for a week.

Study this bar graph of their reading and answer the questions below.

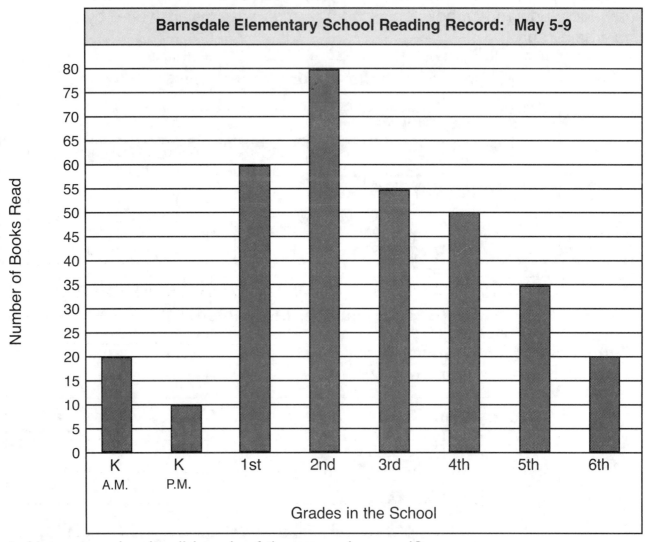

1. How many books did each of these grades read?

   K A.M. _____ 1st _____ 3rd_____ 5th _____

   K P.M. _____ 2nd _____ 4th_____ 6th _____

2. Which grade read the most books? _____

3. What two grades read the same number of books? _____

4. Which books do you think are longer, the books kindergartners read or the books sixth graders read? _____

*How many books can you read in a week? Try it! _____

Draw the Bars!

Draw the bars to show how many hours a week five children spend playing outside or watching television.

Here is the information you will need to make your bar graph.

Name	Outside	Television
Barbara	8	12
Joe	6	20
Jennifer	14	10
Michael	20	6
Sandra	16	10

Use the colors in the key to make your bar graph.

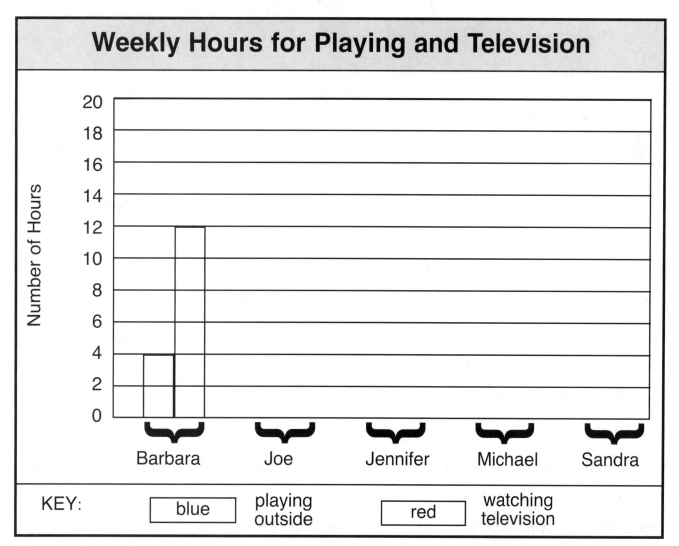

Line Graphs

One type of graph that gives us information is called a *line graph*. A line graph uses dots and lines to show how things change and compare.

Mr. Dean gives five homework assignments each week. He asks his students to graph how many assignments they turn in each week. Here is one of his student's graphs of a six-week period.

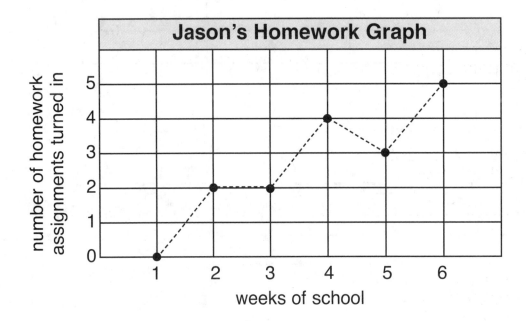

1. How many homework assignments did Jason turn in during each of these weeks?

   week 1 _____ week 3 _____ week 5 _____

   week 2 _____ week 4 _____ week 6 _____

2. What week was his best "homework turned in" week? _____

3. What week was his worst "homework turned in" week? _____

4. Did Jason turn in more homework in the first few weeks or the last few weeks on the graph? _____

*Keep a graph of your homework assignments, too!

Minutes Practiced

Here is a line graph that shows how many minutes a week the Hoopers basketball team practices.

1. On which day do the Hoopers practice the longest?

   _____

2. How many minutes does the team practice in a week?

   _____

3. How many days does the team practice a week?

   _____

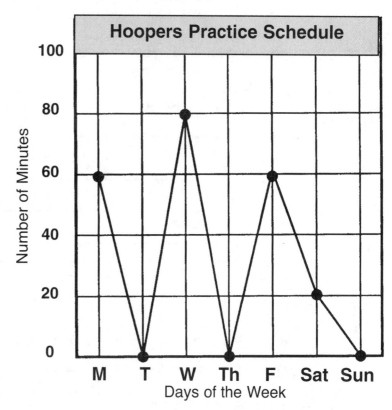

Here is a line graph that compares the practice schedules of the Hoopers and a team called the Dunkers.

1. Which team does not practice on Tuesday?

   _____

2. Which team practices more days a week?

   _____

3. Which team practices more hours a week?

   _____

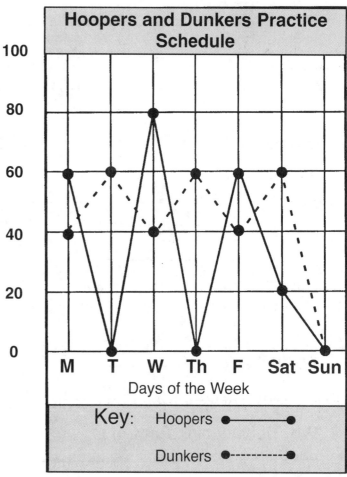

Compare!

Sometimes two different things can be compared on the same line graph. A different color or type of line is used for each thing you want to compare. Graphs with more than one type or color of line are called double line graphs.

Here is a comparison of the number of hours Tony spent outside during two weeks of the same year.

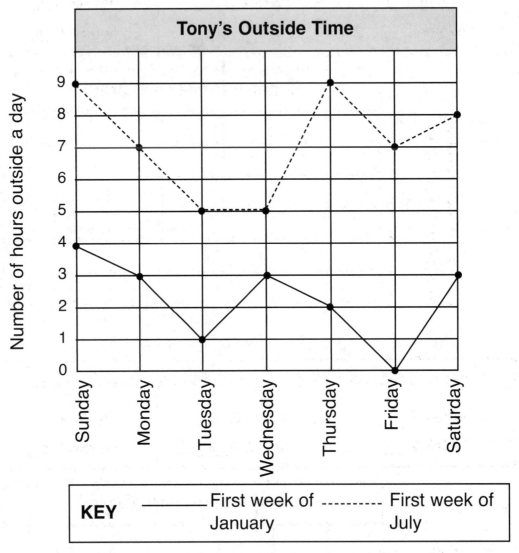

1. How many hours did Tony spend outside on these days?

a. Tuesday, January _____   b. Saturday, July _____

c. Wednesday, July _____   d. Sunday, January _____

e. Monday, January _____   f. Friday, July _____

2. Why do you think Tony spent more time outside in July than he did in January? _____

Connect the Dots

Mr. Dean has two students who have not made graphs of their homework. He wants you to make their graphs. Don't forget to connect the dots!

Here is the information you will need for Susan's graph.

week 1 __3__   week 3 __2__   week 5 __3__

week 2 __3__   week 4 __4__   week 6 __4__

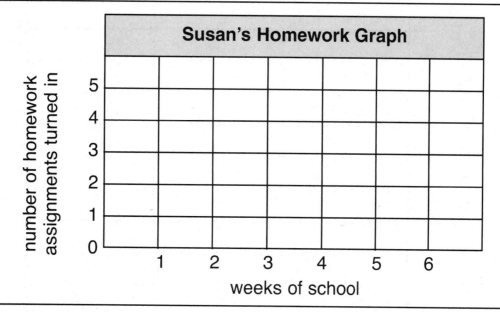

Here is the information you will need for Brian's graph.

week 1 __4__   week 3 __5__   week 5 __5__

week 2 __5__   week 4 __4__   week 6 __5__

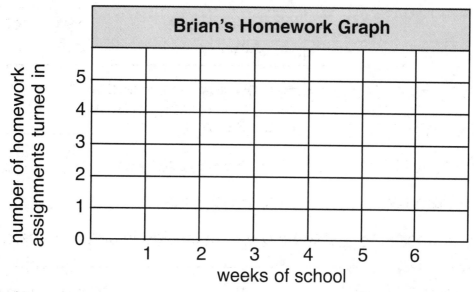

Hidden Prize!

Jim earned a terrific prize for winning first place in the community talent show. The prize he won is spelled out in this graph.

Find the points on the graph that are identified below. Each point you find will give you a letter of the hidden prize. Can you discover the secret?

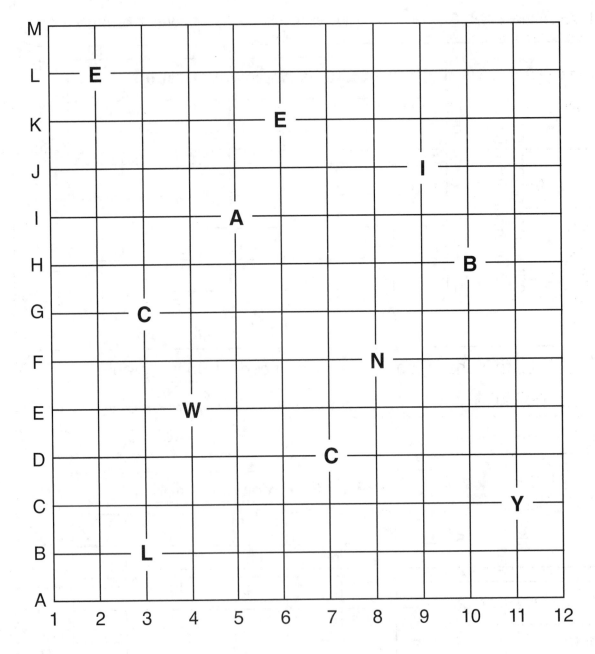

Jim won:

____ ____ ____ ____   ____ ____ ____   ____ ____ ____ ____

5,I   8,F   2,L   4,E   10,H 9,J   3,G   11,C 7,D   3,B   6,K

184

Graph Game

There are some letters of the alphabet hidden in these three graphs. Can you make the dots and draw the lines to find them?

Directions:

1. Begin on the left side of the graph.

2. Match the number in each pair with the number at the bottom. Match the letter in each pair with the letter on the left side of the graph.

3. Mark all the pairs with dots and connect the lines.

4. Write the name of the mystery letter on the line next to the graph.

Mystery Letter #1 _____

Clues:

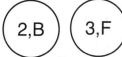 2,B 3,F 4,D 5,F 6,B

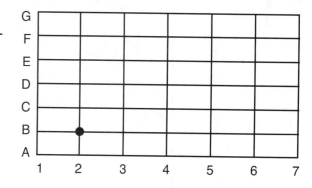

Mystery Letter #2 _____

Clues:

 2,F 3,B 4,D 5,B 6,F

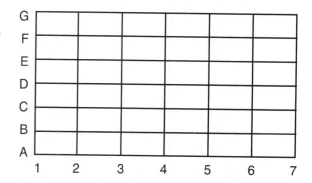

Mystery Letter #3 _____

Clues:

 2,F 4,B 6,F

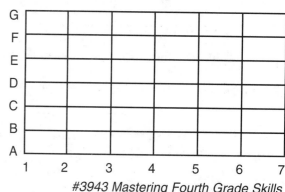

185   #3943 Mastering Fourth Grade Skills

Venn Diagram

A **Venn diagram** is a type of diagram that uses circles to show how things are related to each other. The overlapping parts of the circles show what things the circles have in common.

> Look at this diagram of the activities of two kindergarten classes that share the same room.

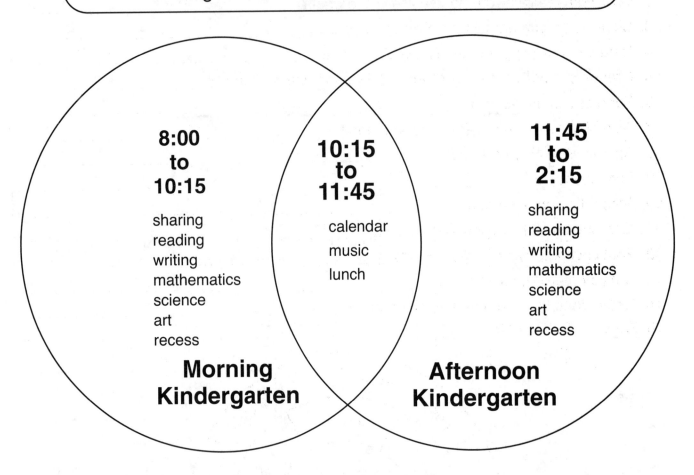

8:00 to 10:15

sharing
reading
writing
mathematics
science
art
recess

Morning Kindergarten

10:15 to 11:45

calendar
music
lunch

11:45 to 2:15

sharing
reading
writing
mathematics
science
art
recess

Afternoon Kindergarten

1. By reading this diagram, can you tell what time of day the two classes are together in the same room? _____ What time? _____

2. What activities do both classes do together?

_____ _____ _____

3. What activities do the classes each do by themselves?

_____ _____ _____

_____ _____ _____

_____

Native American Life

Settlers who came to America saw that Native Americans respected the environment and tried to live in harmony with nature. Native Americans believed that the land was made for all people and that it should be shared. Use the answers in the circles to fill in the blanks. Cross off each answer as you use it. The answer that is left in the circles will complete the bonus sentence.

1. Shelter made of buffalo hide _____
2. Common weapon used by hunters and warriors _____
3. Shiny items purchased from European traders _____
4. Nature's greatest gift to the Native Americans _____
5. Groups of Native Americans who followed the herds of buffalo _____
6. Form of communication _____
7. Animal used for shelter, clothing, and food _____
8. Animal used for transportation _____
9. Iroquois home _____
10. Steep, flat-topped mountain _____
11. Fish preserved by drying and smoking _____
12. Foot covering made of moose hide _____
13. Native American name for corn _____
14. Native American ceremony to celebrate wealth _____
15. Crop other than corn _____

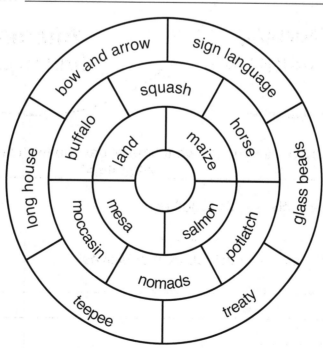

Bonus: An agreement between different governments is called a _____.

The Buffalo

Buffaloes played an important role in the lives of the Plains tribes. Their meat provided food and their hides were used for clothing and shelter. Bowstrings and sewing equipment were made from buffalo sinew. Bones were crafted into cooking utensils and toys for the children.

Rawhide was made into lacings, moccasin soles, and parfleches. (Parfleches were skin pouches that were used to carry small utensils and dried meat.)

Hunting for buffalo was no easy task. At first the Native Americans hunted on foot and shot the animals with bows and arrows. Sometimes hunters would wear a buffalo or wolf skin to mask their human scent so they could get closer to the buffaloes to shoot them. Scouts were sent out to find the herds. Then the hunters lined up in two columns and waved blankets to force the herd toward the edge of a cliff. Other times, buffalo were driven into a corral where they were shot with arrows or clubbed to death.

When Native Americans acquired horses and guns, hunting buffalo became easier. They developed their skills as riders and marksmen. They also became more wasteful and would kill buffalo for sport following in the ways of the white man.

After you have read the paragraph above, write the answers to the clues below. The letters in the boxes will then spell out another name for the American bison.

1. These were made from sinew. □ __ __ __ __ __ __ __ __ __ __

2. They were sent to find the herd __ __ __ □ __ __

3. Skin pouches used to carry meat. __ __ __ □ __ __ __ __ __ __

4. It was worn to hide human scent. __ __ __ □ __ __ __ __

5. These are shot from bows. □ __ __ __ __ __

6. They were waved to
   scare buffaloes. __ □ __ __ __ __ __ __

7. Buffaloes were driven here to
   be shot. __ □ __ __ __ __

Answer: ____ __ __ __ __ __ __ __

188

Native Americans and Horses

Native Americans did not always have horses. It wasn't until the sixteenth century that the Spaniards brought horses to America. At that time, Native Americans still used dogs to carry their packs while hunting. When the Native Americans first saw horses, they called them "big dogs" since they had no word for this new animal in their vocabulary. Southwest Native Americans acquired horses by raiding Spanish settlements. Gradually, they were introduced to the Northern Plains tribes as well. Horses greatly changed the Native American way of life. With horses they could travel faster, carry heavier loads, and hunt more easily. War parties rode horses into battle to raid and fight; escape could be made quickly. In time, the horse became a status symbol. The bridegroom's family gave horses to the parents of the bride. Also, wealth was measured by the number of horses owned.

Read the paragraph above. Then answer the questions.

1. Who brought the first horses to America? _____

_____

2. What was the Native American name for horses? _____

_____

3. Where in America were horses first introduced? _____

_____

4. When was the horse first brought to America? _____

_____

5. Why were horses important to Native Americans? _____

_____

6. How did Native Americans first acquire horses? _____

_____

Challenge:

You are a newspaper reporter. Use your answers to the six questions above to write a news story about the Native American and horses.

Native American Children's Play

Read the paragraphs below and answer the questions.

Native American children's play prepared them for adult roles. Little boys had miniature bows and arrows. They shot at targets on a log. Older boys aimed for the middle of rolling hoops, which trained them to be hunters. Girls had dolls made of cornhusks, corncobs, or wood. They imitated their mothers by taking care of their "babies."

The children did some things just for fun. To make dice, they gathered flat stones, fruit pits, or beaver teeth, and painted a different number of dots on each. They tossed the dice and tried to call the numbers before they landed. They played guessing games, too. Every child took off his or her moccasin and turned around. One child hid a pebble under a shoe, and then everyone tried to guess which shoe had the stone. They also played cat's cradle.

1. A Native American boy shooting at a rolling hoops wanted his arrow to go
   a. through the hoop.
   b. over the hoop.
   c. behind the hoop.

2. A Native American boy was expected to grow up and
   a. win archery contests.
   b. provide meat for his family.
   c. sew clothing.

3. A Native American girl was expected to grow up and
   a. hunt for raccoons.
   b. take care of children.
   c. know how to fish.

4. Today children rarely play
   a. the string game of cat's cradle.
   b. games with dice
   c. with real bows and arrows.

Saving Native American Language & Traditions

Hundreds of years ago the Native Americans lost their lands. The U.S. government moved them to places called reservations. Today one-fifth of all Native Americans live on one. They speak English. This worries some tribe members. They don't want their languages to fade away.

The biggest tribe is the Cherokee. Most live in Oklahoma. Cherokee is their native language. Every person who can speak and understand it is middle aged or older. If their children don't learn it, the language will be gone in less than 50 years.

Parents in the Cherokee and Mohawk tribes formed schools. In these schools students learn the same things that you do. But they learn in their native tongues. They speak Cherokee or Mohawk all day. In gym class they do traditional tribal songs and dances.

1. How did the Native Americans lose their lands hundreds of years ago?
   a. The Native Americans gave land away to anyone who asked for it.
   b. Settlers and the government took the land away, piece by piece.
   c. The Native Americans moved away, and when they returned, other people owned the land.

2. The word "Mohawk" stands for the name of a Native American
   a. song and dance.
   b. ceremony.
   c. tribe and language.

3. In the U.S. today the Native American tribe with the most members is the
   a. the Cherokee.
   b. the Mohawk.
   c. not given in the article.

4. Before starting the school, why did people fear that the Cherokee language would disappear in 50 years?
   a. The people will lose their memories in 50 years.
   b. By then everyone who knows the language will have died.
   c. The government will forbid people to learn second languages.

Colonial Comparisons

State population refers to the number of people living in that state. Every ten years, government officials count how many people are living in each state. They use this information to fund public programs and to determine how many representatives each state requires in Congress. The area of a state refers to how large it is. Alaska is the largest state in the nation, with 615,240 square miles. Rhode Island is the smallest state, with only 1,231 square miles.

Activity

Study the population and area totals for the 13 original colonies. Rewrite the information as two lists in order from the lowest area and population to the highest.

States	Area (in square miles)	Population
Connecticut	5,544	3,405,565
Delaware	2,489	783,600
Georgia	59,441	8,186,453
Maryland	12,407	5,296,486
Massachusetts	10,555	6,349,097
New Hampshire	9,351	1,235,786
New Jersey	8,722	8,414,350
New York	54,475	18,976,457
North Carolina	53,821	8,049,313
Pennsylvania	46,058	12,281,054
Rhode Island	1,545	1,048,319
South Carolina	32,007	4,012,012
Virginia	42,769	7,078,515

Area

1._____
2._____
3._____
4._____
5._____
6._____
7._____
8._____
9._____
10._____
11._____
12._____
13._____

Population

1._____
2._____
3._____
4._____
5._____
6._____
7._____
8._____
9._____
10._____
11._____
12._____
13._____

Extended Activity

- Use an encyclopedia or the Internet to find out how many representatives your state gets in Congress.

Split Proverbs

Benjamin Franklin began printing *Poor Richard's Almanac* in 1733. The little book contained many clever sayings that offered good advice for successful living. Many of these sayings are still quoted today. Complete these proverbs with phrases from the box.

1. Have you something to do tomorrow,_____ .

2. A true friend is _____ .

3. No gain, _____ .

4. Be always ashamed to _____ .

5. People who are wrapped up in themselves make _____ .

6. A penny saved is _____ .

7. Early to bed and early to rise, makes a man _____ .

8. 'Tis easier to prevent bad habits than _____ .

9. An ounce of prevention is worth _____ .

10. A bird in the hand is worth _____ .

a penny earned

two in the bush

catch thyself idle

the best possession

a pound of cure

healthy, wealthy, and wise

without pain

to break them

small packages

do it today

Coded Quotes

Abraham Lincoln was a great leader and orator. Match each number to its letter to decode some of Lincoln's famous words.

A	B	C	D	E	F	G	H	I	J	K	L	M	N	O	P	Q	R	S	T	U	V	W	X	Y	Z
1	2	3	4	5	6	7	8	9	10	11	12	13	14	15	16	17	18	19	20	21	22	23	24	25	26

1. "1   8 -15-21-19 -5   4-9-22-9-4-5-4   1-7-1-9-14-19-20   9-20-19-5-12-6

   "___ _____   _____   _____   _____

   3-1-14-14-15-20   19-20-1-14-4."

   _____ _____."

2. "6-1-9-18   16-12-1-25   9-19   1   10-5-23-5-12."

   "_____   _____   _____   __   _____."

3. "23-15-18-11   23-15-18-11   23-15-18-11   9-19   20-8-5

   "_____,   _____,   _____   _____   _____

   13-1-9-14   20-8-9-14-7."

   _____   _____."

4. "6-15-21-18   19-3-15-18-5   1-14-4   19-5-22-5-14

   "_____   _____   ____   _____

   25-5-1-18-19   1-7-15...."

   _____   _____...."

Flag Etiquette

The United States flag has seven red and six white stripes, which represent the original 13 colonies. There is a star for each of the 50 states on the blue rectangle called the union. The Federal Flag Code is a set of rules for displaying the flag. Here are some of the rules:

- The flag should never be displayed with the union down, except as a signal of distress or danger to life or property.
- The flag should never touch the ground or water.
- The flag should never be displayed or stored in a way that it could be torn, soiled, or damaged.
- The flag, when it is in such condition that it can no longer be displayed, should be destroyed in a dignified way, usually by burning.
- When the national anthem is played and the flag is displayed, all people should face the flag and salute or cover their hearts.
- No other flag should be placed above the flag of the United States of America. If both flags are on the same level, the American flag should appear on the left side.
- The flag of the United States of America should fly at the center and at the highest point when grouped with a number of other flags on staffs.
- When displayed either horizontally or vertically against a wall, the union should be on the observer's left.

Activity

Read the sentences and fill in the blanks.

1. The flag should never touch the ___ ___ ⓞ ___ ___.___
2. No other _f_ ___ _a_ Ⓞ should ever be displayed above the U. S. flag.
3. When displayed ___ ___ ___ ___ ___ ___ ___ Ⓛ ___ _y_, the union should be on the upper left.
4. The flag should never be _t_ Ⓞ ___ _n_ or soiled.
5. A flag in poor condition should be ___ ___ ___ ___ ⓡ Ⓞ ___ ___ ⓓ by burning.
6. The ___ Ⓛ ___ ___ should never be hung with the union down except to show danger.

Arrange the circled letters to spell another name for the flag.

___ ___ ___ ___ ___ ___ ___

Extended Activity

- Here is a list of important days on which to display the flag. Mark these dates on your family's calendar and proudly display your American flag!

Inauguration Day (January 20)

Presidents' Day (third Monday in February)

Armed Forces Day (third Sunday in May)

Memorial Day
(May 30, officially observed the last Monday in May)

Flag Day (June 14)

Independence Day (July 4)

Veterans Day (November 11)

Coming to America

Immigration was not new to the 1920s, but the complexion for the situation changed dramatically in the early part of the twentieth century. From its earliest years the United States of America had an open door policy toward immigrants, placing few restrictions on the number of people entering this country. It was not until 1882 that the first law was passed banning people from a specific country. The Chinese Exclusion Act forbade Chinese laborers because it was feared that they would work for lower pay. In 1907 a "gentleman's agreement" between the United States and Japan barred Japanese immigrants.

In the early 1900s there were two groups who sought to have the doors closed to certain ethnic members. American laborers feared that they would lose their jobs to new immigrants, who were willing to work for lower wages. A second group believed that the newcomers were inferior. Still, it was not until 1917 that restrictions were in place, preventing 33 different categories of people from obtaining entry to the United States.

Immigration in the 1920s changed in another important way. Prior to 1880, newcomers originated mostly from countries in northern and western Europe. When the immigrant population shifted to southern and eastern European countries, some Americans became alarmed at the customs and languages. World War I placed a temporary halt to the problem as very few people came to America during that period. Once the war ended, the wave of immigrants rose steadily, with over 600,000 people arriving in 1921. With the passage of a new law that same year, immigration was limited by a quota system. The National Origins Act of 1924 established severe quotas for southern and eastern European countries. For example, 100,000 Italians had arrived in one year in the early 1900s, but the new quota limited Italy to 5,082 people per year; Greece was allowed only 307 people per year, while Russia was permitted 2,784 per year. Not until the 1960s, when Lyndon Johnson became president, did those quota laws change.

——— Suggested Activities ———

Respond Have the students respond to this question: Are quota laws for immigration fair or necessary? With the class, discuss some possible solutions for this dilemma.

Charts Divide the students into groups and have them make charts comparing 1920s immigration with current immigration. Include topics such as length of travel, mode of travel, cities of entry, and countries of origin.

References

Do People Grow on Family Trees? by Ira Wolfman (Workman Publishing, 1991).
Teacher Created Resources #234 *Thematic Unit—Immigration.*

Immigrant Statistics

An immigrant is a person who has left his or her homeland and moved to a different country to live. Immigrants have many reasons for moving from country to country. Some of the major causes of immigration are to find better jobs, to seek a better way of life, and to escape persecution, war, starvation, and/or disease.

Complete the questions at the bottom of the page.

Immigrants	Years of Major Immigration	Approximate Number of Immigrants
Irish	1840s and 1850s	$1\frac{1}{2}$ million
Germans	1840s and 1880s	4 million
Poles	1880s and 1920s	1 million
Jews	1880s and 1920s	$2\frac{1}{2}$ million
Mexicans	1910s and 1920s	700,000
Dominicans, Haitians, & Jamaicans	1970s and 1980s	900,000
Vietnamese	1970s and 1980s	500,000

Use the data above and your bar graph to solve the following problems. You may want to use a calculator.

1. How many immigrants are represented in the chart? _____
   Round your answer to the nearest million. _____

   Use the rounded answer to complete problem 2.

2. What percent of the total number of immigrants came from each of the following groups:

   a. Poles? _____

   b. Mexicans? _____

   c. Vietnamese? _____

3. What percent of the total immigrant population represented in the chart arrived in the 1970s and 1980s? _____

World Explorers

The names of explorers have been split into two- or three-letter pieces. The letters of the pieces are in order, but the pieces are scrambled. Put the letters together to identify the explorers. Use the clues and the name bank to help you.

1. RO BE ER VE LI RT CA

   ➭ French explorer _____

2. HE AN ES RN RT DO CO

   ➭ traveled west to Baja California _____

3. JU ON EDE AN PO LE NC

   Spanish explorer _____

4. BA OM AS DI EU RT OL

   ➭ explored Africa _____

5. CH LU RI ER CO STO MB US PH

   ➭ started colonies _____

6. IN MU DEC SA HA EL LA MP

   ➭ explored the United States _____

7. HE DS HU NRY ON

   ➭ sailed from Holland _____

8. JA UES RTI CQ CA ER

   ➭ explored Canada _____

9. FR ANC RO CO ZAR IS PI

   ➭ Spanish explorer _____

10. FE ND GEL INA MA RD LAN

   ➭ died during his expedition _____

Name Bank

Ferdinand Magellan	Juan Ponce de León
Jacques Cartier	Christopher Columbus
Bartolomeu Dias	Samuel de Champlain
Henry Hudson	Robert Cavelier
Francisco Pizarro	Hernando Cortés

Continents and Oceans

This world map shows the four oceans and seven continents. Use the world map below to answer the questions.

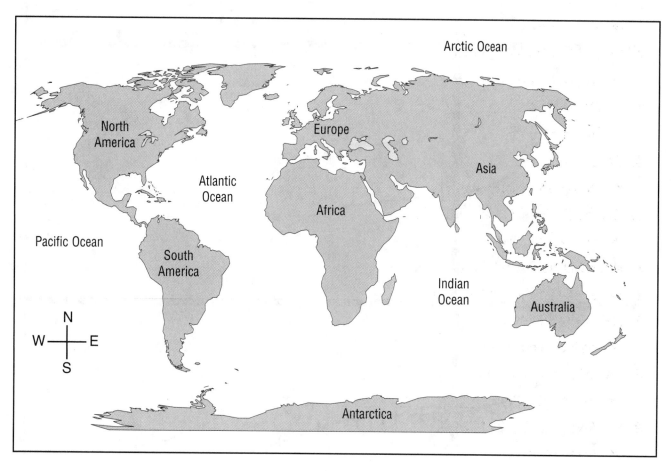

1. What is the name of the continent where you live?_____

2. Which two oceans border South America? _____

3. What ocean is north of Europe? _____

4. Which ocean is east of Africa? _____

5. Which ocean separates North America from Europe? _____

6. Which continent is closest to Antarctica? _____

Map Keys

Use the map below to answer the questions on page 201.

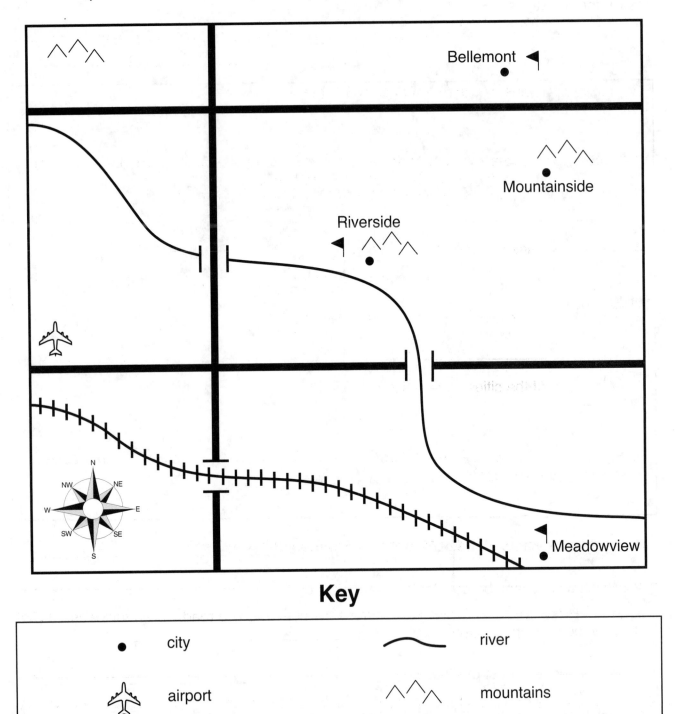

Key

●	city	~~~	river
✈	airport	⌃⌃⌃	mountains
◀	school	▬▬▬	road
| |	bridge	┼┼┼┼	train track

Map Keys *(cont.)*

Use the map on page 200 to answer the questions.

1. How many rivers are shown on this map?

    _____

2. Is the airport closer to the train track or the river?

    _____

3. Start at the mountains in the northwest part of the map. If you traveled along the river, what direction would you be heading? (Use intermediate directions.)

    _____

4. How many cities are shown on the map?

    _____

5. How many of the cities are located near mountains?

    _____

6. How many of the cities have schools in them?

    _____

7. If you were in Bellemont, which direction would you travel to get to the airport? (Use intermediate directions.)

    _____

8. Would it be easier to get to Meadowview by train or by airplane?

    _____

9. Start at Meadowview. Travel north across the river and one road. Then turn west. What city would you find there?

    _____

10. If you were at the airport and wanted to drive to Bellemont, how many bridges would you cross?

    _____

Using Map Grids

Notice the grid on this world map. Use the map and grid to answer the questions on page 203.

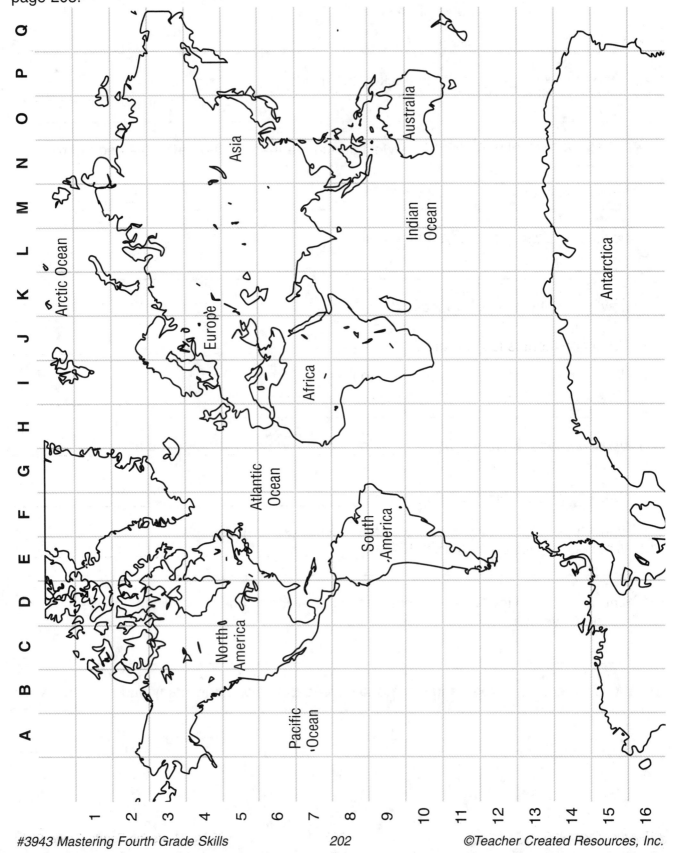

Using Map Grids *(cont.)*

1. What continent is located at 4K? _____

2. What continent is located at 10F? _____

3. If you were at 5C, would you be traveling in a car or in a boat? _____

4. What ocean is located at 8A? _____

5. What continent would you find at 9J? _____

6. What ocean would you find at 11M? _____

7. What continent is located at 3O? _____

8. What continent is located at 10P? _____

9. If you were at 8Q, would you be traveling in a car or in a boat? _____

10. What ocean is located at 1K? _____

11. What continent would you find at 16N? _____

12. What ocean would you find at 6G? _____

How Many Degrees?

The intersection of the Earth's latitude and longitude lines form a grid. All of these lines have degree markings. If you know the degrees of latitude and longitude of a certain place, you can easily find it on a map.

> The map of Colorado below shows the latitude and longitude lines that divide the state. Use the map to answer these questions.

Which city is near:

1. 39° N, 109° W? _____

2. 41° N, 103° W? _____

3. 40° N, 105° W? _____

4. 38° N, 102° W? _____

5. 37° N, 108° W? _____

6. 39° N, 105° W? _____

7. 39° N, 107° W? _____

8. 37° N, 103° W? _____

9. 41° N, 108° W? _____

10. 39° N, 102° W? _____

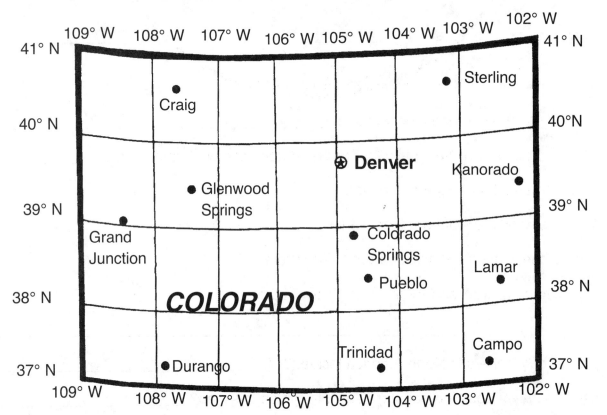

Hemispheres

The Earth is divided into parts called hemispheres. *Hemi* means half. *Sphere* means ball or globe. A hemisphere is half of a globe. An imaginary line called the equator divides the globe into two parts. The part of the Earth that is above the equator is called the Northern Hemisphere. The part that is below the equator is called the Southern Hemisphere.

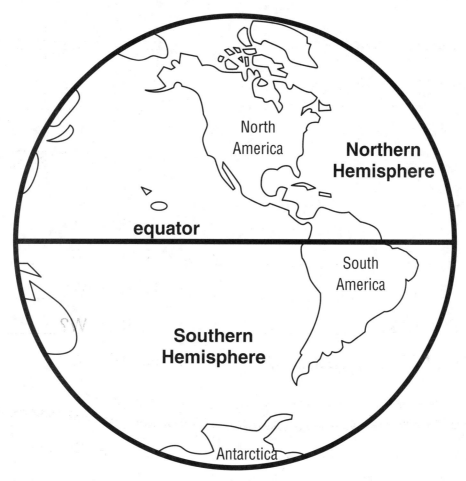

1. What does the word *hemisphere* mean?_____

2. What is the name of the imaginary line that divides the two hemispheres? _____

3. Trace the equator using a red crayon.

4. Draw a star on the Northern Hemisphere.

5. Draw a check mark on the Southern Hemisphere.

6. What two continents shown on this map are in the Southern Hemisphere?

_____

7. In what hemisphere is North America located?_____

8. What continent does the equator pass through on this map?_____

More About Hemispheres

The Earth is divided into Northern and Southern Hemispheres. It is also divided in a way that separates the east from the west. An imaginary line called the prime meridian divides these two hemispheres. These hemispheres are called the Eastern and Western Hemispheres. Use the two halves of a globe below to answer the questions.

Western Hemisphere

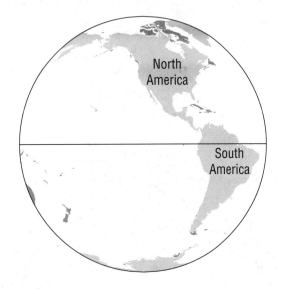

Eastern Hemisphere

1. Europe is in which two hemispheres?

_____

2. South America is in how many hemispheres? Name them.

_____

3. Which two continents lie completely in the Southern Hemisphere?

_____

4. In which two hemispheres do you live?

_____

5. What are all of the continents in the Southern Hemisphere?

_____

6. Which continent is completely in the Northern and Western Hemispheres?

_____

Latitude and Longitude

Like a grid, the lines of latitude and longitude help to locate places on the Earth. If a ship was having trouble at sea, the captain could radio for help and give the latitude and longitude of the ship's location. Using these lines, another plane or ship could come to the rescue.

There are two sets of lines that circle the globe. Lines of latitude run horizontally from east to west. The center line is the equator. Lines of longitude run vertically from north to south. The center line is the prime meridian. These lines are numbered in degrees. For example, a location on the globe might be at 30 degrees north latitude and 120 degrees east longitude.

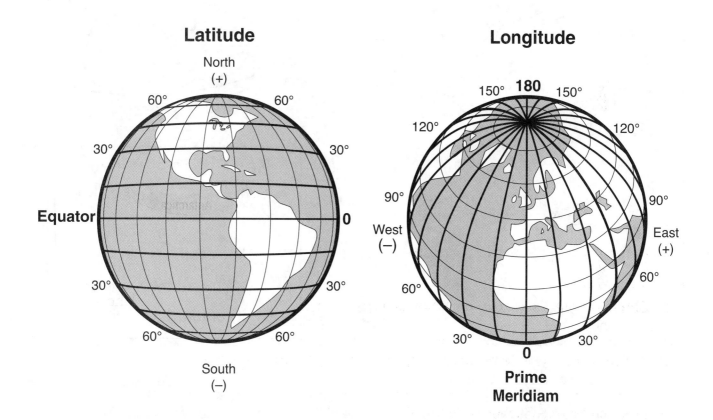

Answer the questions.

1. What are the lines that run from east to west? _____

2. What are the lines that run from north to south? _____

3. For what are the lines of latitude and longitude used? _____

4. What is the center line of latitude?_____

5. What is the center line of longitude? _____

Road Maps

Road maps show the types of roads that are in a specific area. They also tell us other things we may need to know as we plan for travel, such as the distances from town to town, the location of rest areas, and the availability of scenic routes.

> *After you read this map, answer the questions*
> *at the bottom of the page.*

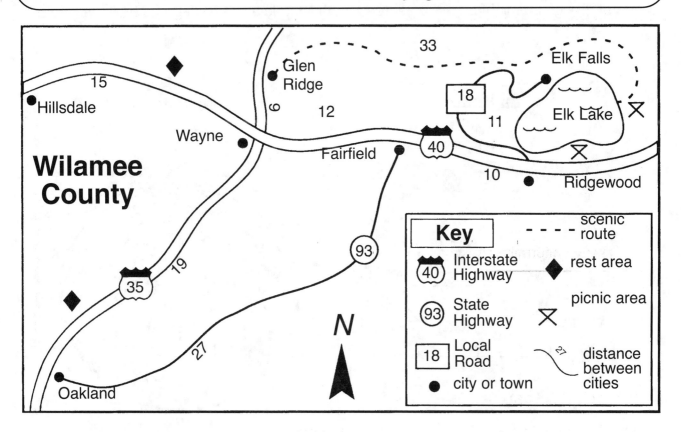

1. Near what highways are the rest areas? _____

2. If you travel on State Highway 93, what is the distance from Oakland to Fairfield?

   _____

3. Interstate Highways 35 and 40 intersect at what city?_____

4. There is a scenic route that ends at the East side of Elk Lake. Where does it
   begin?_____ How long is it? _____

5. What is the distance from Hillsdale to:

   a. Wayne? _____   b. Ridgewood? _____

   c. Fairfield? _____   d. Elk Falls? _____

Political Maps

One type of map that uses boundary lines is called a political map. A political map gives us information about country, province, state, and county boundaries, as well as information about cities, towns, highways, roads, forest areas, and points of interest. Political maps also show oceans, rivers, and lakes, but they do not show the elevations of the land area as physical maps do.

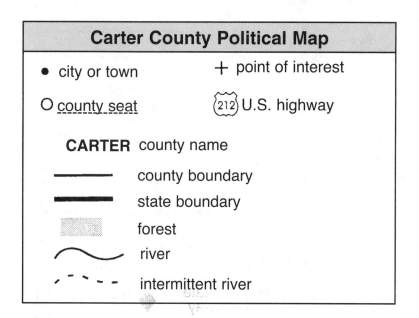

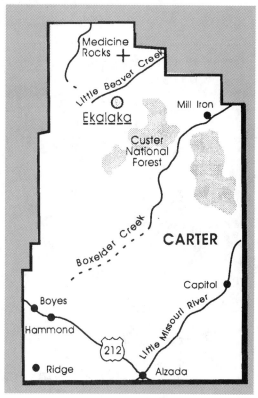

Use this political map of Carter County, Montana, to answer the questions below.

1. Which sides of Montana's border does Carter County help form? _____

   _____

2. What is the name of the county seat? _____

3. Through what three cities does the U.S. highway pass? _____

   _____

4. Name the intermittent river in Carter County. _____

5. What is the point of interest in this county? _____

> *On a separate piece of paper, make a political map of the county in which you live.*

Weather Maps

There are many different kinds of weather maps. Some weather maps show high or low temperatures. Some show where it is snowing, raining, or where the sun is shining. Some weather maps even show the places where pollen is affecting people with allergies!

Use the weather map below to answer the questions about weather in Canada.

1. In which provinces is it sunny? _____

2. In which provinces is it snowy? _____

3. What two kinds of weather are in British Columbia? _____

4. What is another province that is having two kinds of weather? _____

5. What is the weather like in Saskatchewan? _____

6. What is the weather like in the northern part of Quebec? _____

Snacks

I get hungry sometimes when it is not breakfast, lunch, or dinner time. I want a snack!

Some snack foods are not good for my body. These snacks have too much sugar, fat, or salt, like candy and chips.

Some snack foods are great for my body. These foods have many nutrients my body needs. Some good snack foods are fruit, vegetables, and nuts.

I must be very careful when I eat snacks between meals. I must try to eat food that helps my body grow healthy!

Use the word box to help you write the names of "Good Snack Foods."

celery	apple
orange	cheese
nuts	pear
bread	tomato
grapes	carrot

1. _n_ __ __ __

2. __ _p_ _p_ __ __

3. __ __ __ __ __ _y_

4. __ __ _e_ _e_ __

5. __ __ _r_ _r_ __

6. _g_ __ __ __ __ _s_

7. __ _r_ __ __ __ _e_

8. _b_ __ __ __ __

9. __ __ __ _r_

10. _t_ __ __ __ __ _o_

Food Groups

Directions: These words name the food groups. Solve the code and figure out the words. Then draw a line to match each food group with something found in that group.

> **Hint:** The "l" always stands for "e." The "p" always stands for "s." Fill in all the letters in the words below using the letters from the example. As you figure out each letter, write it everywhere it appears. The **&** sign is not in the code.

Example:

v	e	g	e	t	a	b	l	e	s
c	**l**	**q**	**l**	**a**	**h**	**i**	**v**	**l**	**p**

1. __ __ __ __ __
   k h s o f

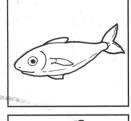

2. __ __ __ __ __ __
   m o b s a p

3. __ __ __ __ &
   w l h a

   __ __ __ __
   m s p r

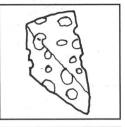

4. __ __ __ __ __ &
   i o l h k

   __ __ __ __ __
   z h p a h

5. __ __ __ __ &
   m h a p

   __ __ __ __ __ __
   p d l l a p

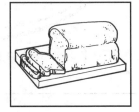

Eating Right

To have a balanced diet, you should think about what to eat at each meal. For example, you should have more servings of vegetables than meat or fish.

Directions: Use the clue below each plate to find the word hidden on the plate. Write it on the line below the plate. The letters of each word can go to the right and down. The first one is done for you.

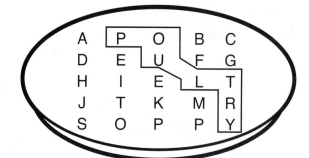

Example: another name for chicken

poultry

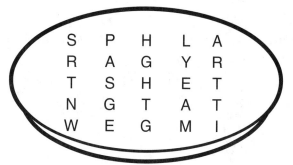

3. a type of pasta

_____

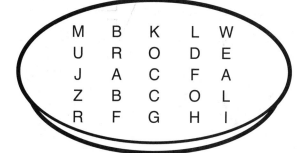

1. a vegetable

_____

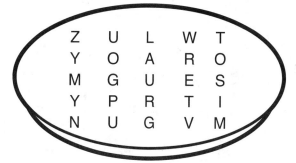

4. made from milk

_____

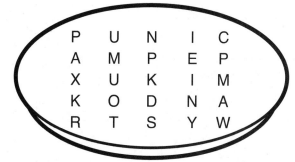

2. a fruit used in pie

_____

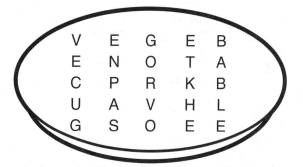

5. tomato juice

_____

Nutrition Word Search

Eating good foods will keep you healthy. These words are all related to nutrition:

eggs	protein	calories	oils	nuts	corn
milk	energy	fish	fats	bread	meal
meat	sugar	fruit	vitamin	mineral	

Directions: Find and circle the words in the word search.   They go down and across.

```
n  c  a  l  o  r  i  e  s  a  r
u  o  p  e  n  e  r  g  y  b  e
t  r  r  m  a  s  u  g  a  r  m
s  n  o  e  l  o  l  s  f  e  i
v  i  t  a  m  i  n  e  r  a  l
y  g  e  l  e  l  o  o  u  d  k
d  a  i  p  a  s  p  f  i  s  h
e  t  n  i  t  t  f  a  t  s  e
```

Bonus: Copy the letters that were not used in the word search in order from left-to-right and top to bottom. Then answer this question:

What do most people like to have, yet everyone wants to get rid of as soon as getting it?

__ __ __ __ __ __ __ __ __ __ __ __ __ __

__ __ __ __ __ __ __ __ __ __ __

Health Proverb

Directions: A proverb is a wise saying. To find the proverb, follow these steps:

- The letters below each go in the blank squares above them.
- A black space shows the end of a word.
- Do the short words first.
- A few letters have already been placed for you.

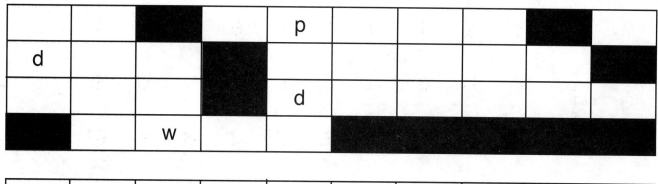

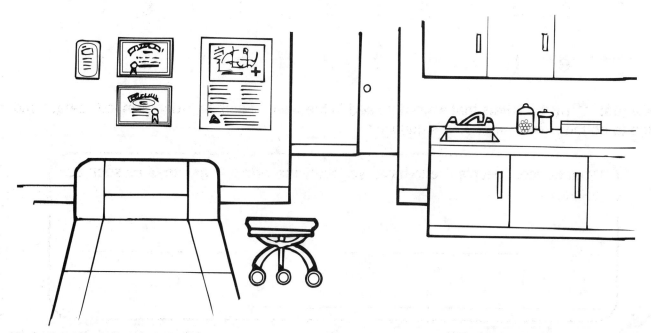

Science

Peanut Products

By the time George Washington Carver died in 1943, he had found over 300 uses for the common peanut. Listed below are just a few of his discoveries. You will have to unscramble the letter groups to learn what they are. Use the Peanut Box to help you.

1. turbet   ____ ____ ____ ____ ____ ____

2. asop   ____ ____ ____ ____

3. kni   ____ ____ ____

4. leacre   ____ ____ ____ ____ ____ ____

5. lsctipas   ____ ____ ____ ____ ____ ____ ____ ____

6. eaprp   ____ ____ ____ ____ ____

7. acbleh   ____ ____ ____ ____ ____ ____

8. lmki   ____ ____ ____ ____

9. eysd   ____ ____ ____ ____

10. dncya   ____ ____ ____ ____ ____

11. tmea ucsae   ____ ____ ____ ____   ____ ____ ____ ____ ____

12. edrdi focfee   ____ ____ ____ ____ ____   ____ ____ ____ ____ ____ ____

Peanut Box

plastics	dried coffee	candy
bleach	meat sauce	ink
dyes	milk	soap
butter	cereal	paper

Body Systems Solve It!

Your body has a group of systems that work together to keep you breathing, thinking, and moving. Eating good food and exercising helps your body systems do their jobs.

Directions: Choose a word from the box that matches the clue. Fill in the puzzle.

> respiratory   skeletal   endocrine   circulatory
>
> digestive   x-ray   nervous   muscular

1. This system forms a frame for your body. __ __ __ __ __ __ __ __

2. If you break a bone, your doctor orders this kind of picture. __ __ __ __ __

3. This system lets you think, feel, move, see, and hear. __ __ __ __ __ __ __

4. This one moves blood through your body. __ __ __ __ __ __ __ __ __ __ __

5. This system has glands that make tears and sweat. __ __ __ __ __ __ __ __ __

6. This system moves air through your lungs. __ __ __ __ __ __ __ __ __ __ __

7. This one lets your turn your head, walk, and lift a cup. __ __ __ __ __ __ __ __

8. This one lets your body use the food that you eat. __ __ __ __ __ __ __ __ __

The Brain

The human brain is the one feature that truly sets people apart from other animals. Our brains are three or four times larger than most mammals of our size.

Different areas of the brain control various bodily functions such as breathing, thirst, and heartbeat. Unscramble the letter groups to find the names of the different brain parts. Use the Word Box to help you.

Word Box

medulla	cerebellum	pons
spinal cord	midbrain	cerebrum

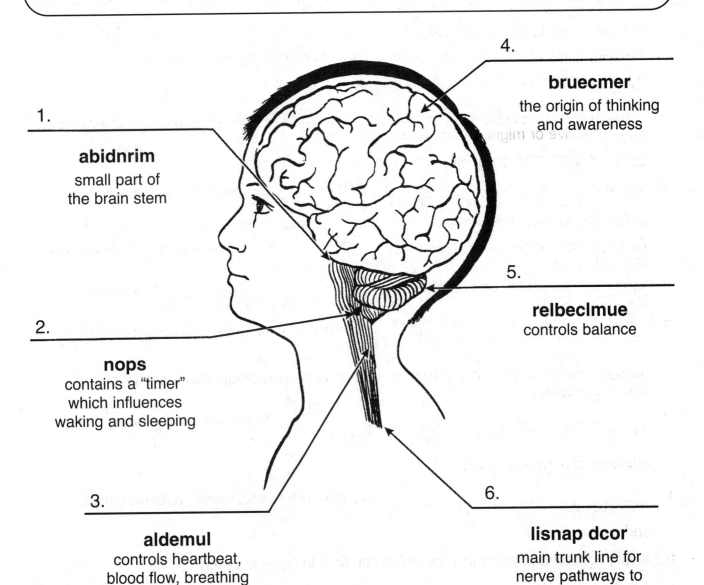

4.

bruecmer
the origin of thinking
and awareness

1.

abidnrim
small part of
the brain stem

5.

relbeclmue
controls balance

2.

nops
contains a "timer"
which influences
waking and sleeping

3.

aldemul
controls heartbeat,
blood flow, breathing

6.

lisnap dcor
main trunk line for
nerve pathways to
and from the brain

Volcano Facts

Directions: Discover some interesting facts about volcanoes as you solve the problems. Use the code to solve the puzzle statements below.

A = 26 x 12 _____   J = 38 + 52 _____   S = 512 ÷ 16 _____

E = 16 x 11 _____   N = 77 + 19 _____   W = 1,173 ÷ 51 _____

I = 71 x 3 _____   R = 709 + 51 _____   D = 306 – 105 _____

M = 15 x 5 _____   V = 579 + 47 _____   H = 62 – 13 _____

Q = 39 x 4 _____   Z = 719 + 207 _____   L = 111 – 19 _____

U = 62 x 3 _____   C = 156 ÷ 13 _____   P = 999 – 555 _____

Y = 20 x 41 _____   G = 189 ÷ 9 _____   T = 818 – 319 _____

B = 627 + 11 _____   K = 104 ÷ 8 _____   X = 638 – 547 _____

F = 38 + 73 _____   O = 70 ÷ 5 _____

1. A ___ ___ ___ ___ ___ ___ ___ is the huge, round crater which forms when the cone
   12 312 92 201 176 760 312
   of a live volcano collapses inward.

2. An instrument which can pinpoint the position of rising magma is called a
   ___ ___ ___ ___ ___ ___ ___ ___ ___ ___ ___ .
   32 176 213 32 75 14 75 176 499 176 760

3. A special branch of geology that specializes in the study of volcanoes, especially those
   that are active or might become active, is called
   ___ ___ ___ ___ ___ ___ ___ ___ ___ ___ ___ .
   626 14 92 12 312 96 14 92 14 21 820

4. Volcanic ___ ___ ___ ___ ___ ___ ___ ___ ___ only began to be studied seriously
   176 760 186 444 499 213 14 96 32
   in the late nineteenth century.

5. Changes in a volcano are caused by ___ ___ ___ ___ ___ moving toward the surface
   to erupt.   75 312 21 75 312

6. Volcanoes are also found on other ___ ___ ___ ___ ___ ___ ___ like Mars and
   Mercury.   444 92 312 96 176 499 32

7. ___ ___ ___ ___ ___ ___ ___ ___ ___ eruptions of sticky, stiff lava commonly
   176 91 444 92 14 32 213 626 176

   produce one or more of these fragmental deposits: pyroclastic flows, ash falls, and
   volcanic mudflows.

8. ___ ___ ___ ___ ___ ___ ___ ___ ___ ___ ___ flows consist of glowing, hot
   444 820 760 14 12 92 312 32 499 213 12

   mixtures of pumice and ash.

9. ___ ___ ___ ___ ___ ___ ___ ___ are mixtures of fragmental, volcanic debris
   75 186 201 111 92 14 23 32
   and water.

10. A very light type of volcanic rock which can float in water is called
    ___ ___ ___ ___ ___ ___ .
    444 186 75 213 12 176

Birth of an Island

Read the passage below and answer the questions.

Volcanoes change the Earth's surface. Surtsey, the world's newest land mass, started as an undersea volcano. The volcano spilled lava on the sea floor. The lava cooled to form rock. Over a long time the lava built up until it became a mountain. When it reached the sea's surface, it formed the island. All of the Hawaiian Islands formed this same way.

Surtsey appeared in 1963 near Iceland, another volcanic island. Sailors at sea saw the huge cloud of smoke and steam rising from the sea. Lava flowed for three and a half years. When it stopped, Surtsey was a mile wide.

The people of Iceland chose the name Surtsey for the new island. In their legends it is the fire god's name. Fire gave birth to the island.

1. How do you think the sailors who saw the birth of Surtsey felt?
   a. sad
   b. surprised
   c. angry

2. Which one is not a volcanic island?
   a. Hawaii
   b. Iceland
   c. Long Island

3. Surtsey is named for which legendary figure?
   a. the god of fire
   b. the goddess of water
   c. the god of islands

4. What do you think the land mass called Surtsey looks like today?
   a. farmland
   b. rocky
   c. sandy

The Great San Francisco Earthquake

Read the passage below and answer the questions.

On April 18, 1906, at 5:13 A.M, a strong earthquake shook 290 miles along a fault line. Part of the fault ran through San Francisco. Buildings collapsed. A train in the station fell over. Hundreds of frightened dogs fled the city.

Fires broke out. Even worse, the water pipes were wrecked. Without a steady supply of water, firemen could do little to fight the blazes. In desperation they blew up whole blocks of buildings to stop the flames from spreading. For three days the fires raged. In the end more than 28,000 buildings were gone. A quarter of a million people had no shelter. About 3,000 lives were lost.

Another strong earthquake hit the city in 1989, but this time just 12 people died. People had learned from the past. They had built buildings that could endure earthquakes.

1. How many years passed between the Great San Francisco Earthquake and the next strong quake?
   a. 18 years
   b. 12 years
   c. 83 years

2. Why did the dogs leave the city?
   a. They went to warn the people in the countryside about the quake.
   b. They were terrified and wanted to get away from the disaster.
   c. They went to find help for the people of San Francisco.

3. How did the water pipes get broken?
   a. They broke open from the ground's movement.
   b. They were crushed by the falling rocks.
   c. They were old and hadn't been maintained.

4. The word *desperation* means feeling
   a. afraid of fire.
   b. there's no other choice.
   c. angry.

Seismic Search

Fill in the sentences below, and then locate the underlined words in the word search. Words may go up, down, or horizontally. Use the word bank below for help.

1. The earth's outer layer is called its _____ .

2. The San Andreas Fault is found in _____ .

3. A _____ is a crack in the earth's crust between two plates.

4. A huge piece of the earth's crust is called a _____ .

5. When two plates collide, there is an _____ .

6. The earth's plates are made of _____ .

7. The earth's plates are constantly _____ .

8. The ground _____ during an earthquake.

Word Bank

moving   plate
fault   shakes
earthquake   crust
rock   California

c	f	a	h	e	d	g	s	g	h	c	o	s	k	e	d	s	k	o	g
g	a	g	h	k	o	e	d	k	j	r	e	o	w	l	d	h	k	e	d
p	u	b	m	e	d	i	g	u	e	u	p	l	a	t	e	a	l	m	d
o	l	w	l	k	n	g	i	o	e	s	w	c	k	d	i	k	q	i	e
b	t	w	d	g	i	e	e	a	r	t	h	q	u	a	k	e	g	h	i
j	x	z	c	m	d	k	o	e	c	l	w	p	w	d	d	s	l	o	p
c	a	l	i	f	o	r	n	i	a	w	p	l	e	m	g	d	o	p	s
b	s	o	p	d	v	v	w	p	d	l	k	b	o	d	s	j	o	p	w
w	o	p	d	m	g	o	i	s	g	p	i	n	d	s	i	n	p	g	s
w	o	p	s	g	k	b	s	n	w	g	s	o	i	n	r	o	c	k	s
q	w	u	i	r	o	x	d	m	g	b	s	p	o	i	n	g	s	i	t

Electricity Facts

Directions: Solve each problem below. Then write the answer in the blank to find out some interesting facts about electricity.

1. 932 + 963	The world's first hydroelectric A.C. generating plant began operation at Niagara Falls, New York, in _____ .
2. 1288 + 687	One of the nation's largest solar heating and cooling systems has been in operation since _____ at the George A. Towns Elementary School in Atlanta, Georgia.
3. 100 x 20 = ___	"Solar One," a solar power test plant near Barstow, California, has _____ mirrors which reflect solar heat to a central receiver, producing steam to operate an electricity-producing turbine.
4. 479 − 359	To make electricity, we must push electrons through a circuit. It takes pressure. We measure electric pressure in volts. The electric pressure in your home is probably _____ volts.
5. 101 − ___ = 86	Amperes measure how much electricity is being pushed through a circuit. Some wires can safely carry _____ amperes.
6. 100 ÷ 5 = ___	Watts measure the amount of electric power we are using to run machines, light a lamp, etc. A small light bulb uses a little electric power, possibly a _____ watt bulb.
7. 250 x 4	Kilowatt is a large amount of electric power. One kilowatt = _____ watts. Big electric kitchen stoves can use 10 kilowatts of power.
8. 258 + 179	In western Kentucky, there is a large fuel-powered steam generating plant. There are three _____ foot high cooling towers.
9. 51 + ___ = 66	If a wire in your circuit carries as much as _____ amperes of electricity, then you need a fuse to protect your circuit of amperes.

Electric Appliances

Although Thomas Edison is credited with the invention of the electric light bulb, he invented or improved many other items which enhance our lives today. For example, Edison invented the power systems that bring electricity to homes through wires. In addition, he invented the circuits and switches that allow us to turn electricity on and off.

Imagine what your day would be like without the many electrical gadgets to which you have become accustomed. Listed below are just a few of the modern conveniences that use electricity. Write each name in the puzzle. Some letters are provided to help you get started. When you have completed the puzzle, answer the questions at the bottom of the page.

Electric Appliances

hair dryer	skillet	television	can opener
stereo	refrigerator	stove	coffee maker
telephone	computer	blender	VCR
video games	radio	clock	microwave oven

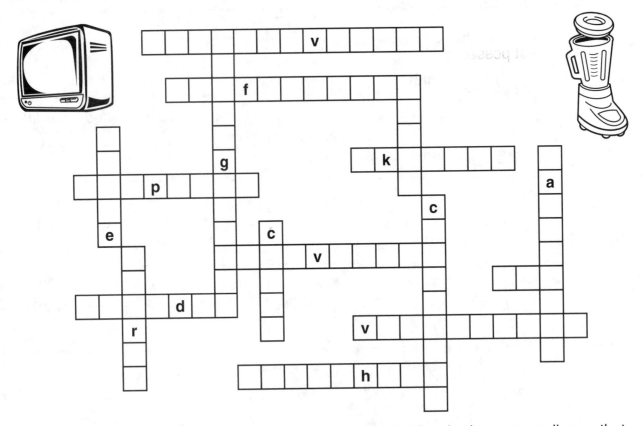

Which of these appliances do you have in your home? What is the one appliance that you cannot do without? Why? _____

_____

_____

It's Raining Words!

The cloud below is raining weather words. Find the words written on the cloud in the word search. All of the words are printed straight down or straight across.

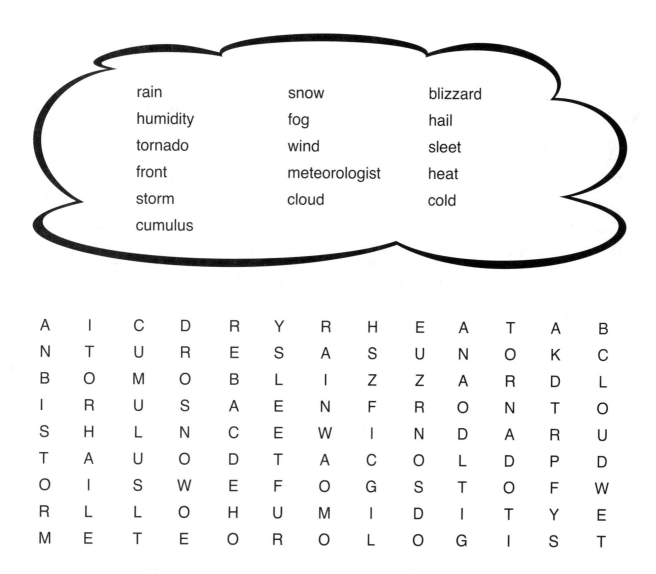

rain	snow	blizzard
humidity	fog	hail
tornado	wind	sleet
front	meteorologist	heat
storm	cloud	cold
cumulus		

```
A  I  C  D  R  Y  R  H  E  A  T  A  B
N  T  U  R  E  S  A  S  U  N  O  K  C
B  O  M  O  B  L  I  Z  Z  A  R  D  L
I  R  U  S  A  E  N  F  R  O  N  T  O
S  H  L  N  C  E  W  I  N  D  A  R  U
T  A  U  O  D  T  A  C  O  L  D  P  D
O  I  S  W  E  F  O  G  S  T  O  F  W
R  L  L  O  H  U  M  I  D  I  T  Y  E
M  E  T  E  O  R  O  L  O  G  I  S  T
```

Bonus: In the word search there are three weather-related words that weren't listed. Each one is three letters long. Can you find them?

_____   _____   _____

Weather Report

Hidden in each sentence below is a word that a meteorologist might use in a weather report. Each "weather word" will be formed as either

- a part of a word *or*

- by combining the end of one word with the beginning of the next.

Directions: Underline the weather word in each sentence. Then write it on the line.

Sentence	Weather Word
Example: The taco was too spi<u>cy</u>.	icy
Example: Alo<u>ha I</u>lene.	hail
1. Alex is now working at the mall.	
2. We found mildew around the tub in the bathroom.	
3. I can hold my breath under water for two minutes.	
4. Robert is unlikely to win the race.	
5. Ann sprained her ankle falling off her skateboard.	
6. According to Eric, loud is the only way to sing!	
7. Wouldn't it be fun to sail the seas on a ship?	
8. Dad had to scold Chris for disobeying.	
9. Please rewind the tape.	
10. Do you like cinnamon spice applesauce?	

The Red Planet

Read the passage below and answer the questions.

Astronomers on Earth can see the details on the reddish surface of Mars. Other than Earth, Mars is the only planet with possible evidence that it may have once sustained life. Today, nothing appears to live there.

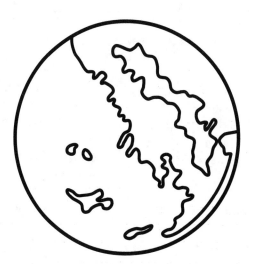

As the fourth planet from the sun, Mars is our next-door neighbor in the solar system. It's about half the size of our Earth. Yet it has some gigantic features. It has a canyon that's the same length as the distance between New York City and San Francisco. One extinct volcano towers more than twice as high as the tallest mountain on Earth.

Mars is very cold. Its lowest known temperature is -191°F. The highest known temperature is only -24°F. Brr! It doesn't sound like a good substitute for Earth.

1. Why is Mars so much colder than Earth?

    a. It is half the size of Earth.
    b. It is farther away from the sun.
    c. Nothing lives there.

2. Compared to Mars' canyon, our Grand Canyon is

    a. shorter.
    b. longer.
    c. about the same length.

3. The nickname for Mars is

    a. the Neighbor Planet.
    b. the Canyon Planet.
    c. the Red Planet.

4. The word *sustained* means

    a. ended.
    b. supported.
    c. damaged.

The Planets

Name _____ Date _____

These words appear scrambled in the sentences below. Find them and write the unscrambled words on the lines before the sentences. (Add capitals where necessary.)

Mars	comet	moon	atmosphere	Neptune
Saturn	Mercury	asteroid	solar system	distance
Pluto	Jupiter	Earth	satellite	space
planet	temperature	Uranus	Venus	meteor

_____ 1. The earth has only one *nomo*.

_____ 2. The planet *sarm* is sometimes called the Red Planet.

_____ 3. We have been studying the *roals ytmess*.

_____ 4. The moon is Earth's only *letletais*.

_____ 5. The rings of *runtas* are beautiful to see.

_____ 6. Many science fiction stories have been written about *nuves*.

_____ 7. The *premauteert* of the planets differs widely.

_____ 8. The spacecraft slipped through the *stoidera* belt.

_____ 9. The planet *cerymur* is the closest planet to the sun.

_____ 10. The planet *putjire* is known for its mysterious red spot.

_____ 11. We can't see the surface of Venus because of its thick *photersame*.

_____ 12. What is the *catsnide* between Earth and Mars?

_____ 13. Atronauts travel through *sepac*.

_____ 14. The *teemor* burned up in the atmosphere.

_____ 15. The planet *punntee* was named for the god of the sea.

_____ 16. Earth is a *netalp* of the sun.

_____ 17. Rings were recently discovered around *anurus*.

_____ 18. The planet *optul* is the outermost planet.

_____ 19. Ancient people were afraid when they saw a *tomec* in the night sky.

_____ 20. The planet *thare* is the third planet from the sun.

Earth's Environment

Name _____ Date _____

Match each of these words with its definition.

environment	organic	food web	Earth	air
habitat	pollution	preserve	rain forest	trash
endangered	recycle	waste	landfill	green
food chain	extinct	water	smog	dump

Definitions

_____ 1. the third planet from the sun; our home

_____ 2. at risk of disappearing from the earth

_____ 3. the place where we live; our surroundings

_____ 4. a kind of dump where trash is buried

_____ 5. dirt and smoke in the air; air pollution

_____ 6. to use something over again

_____ 7. no longer in existence; having died out

_____ 8. a safe place reserved for animals; a refuge

_____ 9. an area of ground covered with grass

_____ 10. grown without chemicals; natural

_____ 11. a series of plants and animals that are linked together because they feed on one another

_____ 12. the place where an animal or plant generally lives

_____ 13. the liquid that makes up the oceans, rivers, lakes, etc., of the earth

_____ 14. what we breathe; Earth's atmosphere

_____ 15. a more complicated food chain

_____ 16. what occurs when harmful substances are released into the environment

_____ 17. anything not used; left over from a process

_____ 18. useless stuff that is thrown away

_____ 19. a place to put trash

_____ 20. a region that is always hot and wet, where many trees grow and animals live

Underwater Organisms
Crossword Puzzle

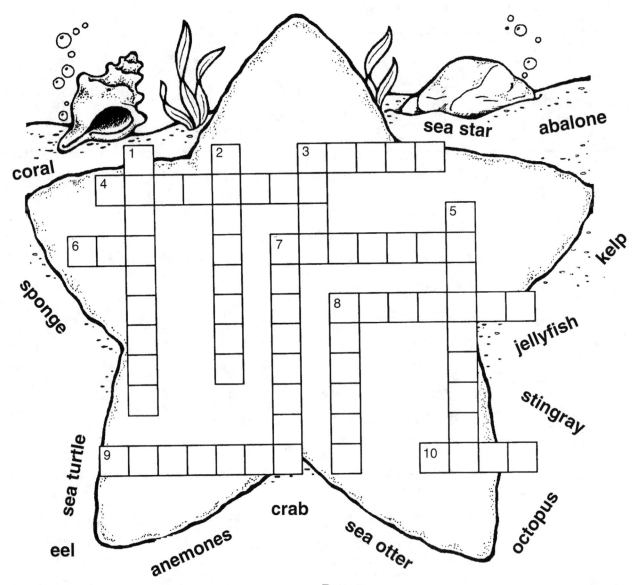

Across

3. A sea animal which resembles a plant
4. This mammal can use a stone to open shellfish.
6. This snake-like creature is electric!
7. A shell that's known for its mother-of-pearl
8. A five-armed animal with hundreds of tube feet
9. This mollusk has eight arms covered with suckers.
10. A kind of seaweed

Down

1. This simple creature stings with its deadly tentacles.
2. A fish with a poisonous dart on the end of its whiplike tail
3. This crustacean's pincers contain edible white meat.
5. A reptile that comes ashore to lay eggs
7. They may look like flowers, but they're really animals.
8. A plant-like sea animal with a porous structure

Answer Key

Page 8

Answers for specific nouns will vary.

1. P, country
2. C, Monday
3. C, January
4. P, day
5. P, month
6. P, planet
7. P, city
8. P, country
9. P, holiday
10. C, Pacific Ocean
11. C, Mt. Washington
12. C, Belgium
13. P, state
14. P, mountain
15. P, lake
16. C, Easter
17. C, Los Angeles
18. C, Jamaica
19. C, Rover
20. C, Jumbo
21. P, car
22. C, Mrs. Lee
23. C, President Bush
24. C, Mayor Bradley
25. C, Earth
26. C, Kennedy Jr. High
27. P, lady/woman
28. P, apple/grandmother
29. C, "America"
30. C, "The Raven"

Page 9

1. twelve
2. five
3. eight
4. seven
5. two
6. four
7–15 (Answers will vary. The following are sample responses.)
7. These, those
8. This, that
9. These, those
10. Those, these
11. its
12. My
13. your
14. Her
15. their, our

Page 10

Helping
1. will
2. is
3. were
4. can
5. has
6. have
7. have
8. will
9. will
10. will

Action
1. ride
2. ridden
3. pushed
4. move
5. driven
6. pulled
7. seen
8. go
9. eat
10. drink

Page 11

1. near
2. there/here
3. here/there
4. out
5. often
6. soon
7. now
8. yesterday
9. harder, hardest
10. softly, most softly
11. good, better
12. easier, easiest
13. fast, fastest

Page 12

sample responses
1. You can wear your blue or black jeans.
2. Your white T-shirt fits better, but your red T-shirt is more colorful.
3. Do you want yellow or pink patches on your jeans?
4. Jillian's T-shirt looks attractive, and/but Jacqueline's jeans are stunning.
5. I have three pairs of blue jeans, but I want another pair.
6. You can wash your old jeans or iron your new jeans.
7. This white T-shirt is mine, and that white T-shirt is yours.
8. Let's wear our blue jeans today and our red jeans tomorrow.
9. My old jeans fit me well, but my new jeans do not.
10. I have washed my new red T-shirt but not my new blue T-shirt.

Page 13

1. When I went to the store, I saw my teacher, Mrs. Roe.
2. My family will go to Disneyland in July.
3. I am reading *Old Yeller* this week.
4. My sister, Sarah, says her favorite subject is Spanish.
5. On Wednesday, we will celebrate Groundhog Day.
6. My brother said that Mom was a cheerleader at Eastside High School.
7. In August, we're going to visit Aunt Mary in San Francisco, California.
8. Benjie had a birthday, and we sang "Happy Birthday to You."
9. My friend Rosa speaks Spanish, and I speak English.
10. My neighbor Julia is going to Paris, France, next June.

Page 14

"Move, David." Standing on the chair, Jonathon reached up to feel the hole. **He** took his bike lock key out of his pocket and tried it in the keyhole.

"That doesn't come close to fitting," David protested. Jonathon got off the chair and pushed it back over the desk. "No," he said, "before I look for a key, I need to know what I'm looking for." He pushed the chair back over to the hole. Then he walked over to the desk, rummaged around, and found a piece of paper and a pencil.

"What are you doing?"

"You'll see." Jonathon climbed back up on the chair, holding the paper and pencil. **He** had to stand on tiptoe to reach the keyhole; even then, he had to reach up and lean his head back—it was most awkward, but he managed to get a key shape traced.

"Now I'm ready to find the key!" **In** his enthusiasm, Jonathon forgot about the midday heat.

He ran down the stairs and banged out the screen door. **David** followed at a more leisurely pace and caught up with Jonathon on the porch.

"Where am I going to look first?" Staring out towards the mulberry tree, **Jonathon** straddled the porch railing and pondered the best place to begin looking for a key. "I know! **I'll** go down and check around the basement."

"**At** least it's cool down there," David said.

Page 15

1. Jerry was born on October 5, 1986.
2. My favorite Christmas was December 25, 1992.
3. Susan's mom came home from the hospital on April 6, 1994.
4. We took our summer vacation on July 21, 1993.
5. My grandfather was born on August 11, 1941.

6. On April 6, 1994, Susan's mom brought a new baby girl home from the hospital.
7. My grandfather remembers July 20, 1969, as an important date in history.
8. On July 21, 1993, my family went to Hawaii for our summer vacation.

Page 16

1. Luke's, couldn't
2. Rosas' weren't
3. Rosa's, wasn't
4. She'll, isn't
5. I've, it'll
6. mother's, daughter's
7. She's, brother's
8. That's, I've
9. would've, couldn't
10. It's, life's
11. else's, shouldn't
12. I'm, it's

Page 17

1. Ryan asked, "What do you want to play, Martha?"
2. Martha answered, "Let's play baseball."
3. "Okay, we'll play baseball first," said Ryan, "but let's play basketball after that."
4. Mom called, "The cookies are ready."
5. "Oh, boy," the boys yelled at the same time, "let's eat!"

Page 18

1. C
2. C
3. X
4. X
5. C
6. X
7. cat's dish
8. dog's treat
9. teacher's desk
10. Kayla Beth's doll
11. horse's oats
12.–15. Answers will vary.

Page 19

1. I: Where did you get that hat?
2. E: Oh, no, the ball's headed this way!
3. D: It's time to go to school.
4. E: There's an octopus on your head!
5. I: Have you seen my pet snake?
6. E: Don't point that at me!
7. D: The sun will be setting at 7:47 tonight.
8. E: We won a trip to Hawaii!
9. I: May I borrow your car?
10. D: Take off your shoes and stay awhile.

Page 20

1. My mother and I will be driving a hundred miles today. It's my grandma's birthday.
2. I have a new puppy. His name is Lollipop.
3. I said, "What are you doing?"
4. Watch out, John!
5. Have you seen my little brother? I think he's lost. (or !)
6. I fell into the pool. My shoes are wet!
7. We saw Mrs. Hunter at Palm Elementary School on Thursday.
8. My friend lives in Northridge, California. She's really funny.
9. Do you like liver?
10. Will you please hold my snake? He's hungry.

Page 21

The two boys went around to the side of the **house**. The cool musty odor of the basement greeted Jonathon as he opened the door. He went down the narrow step **slowly**, allowing his eyes time to adjust to the darkness. Jonathon rounded the post at the bottom of the stairs and glanced at the shelves. He couldn't decide whether or not to search them thoroughly. Deciding not to, he turned around to survey the rest of the basement and almost bumped into David.

"It's too dark to look very well down here," Jonathon said. **"I'll** never find a key in this mess. If I did, it probably would be rusted and corroded and wouldn't **work."** He sighed and went up the stairs as slowly as he had gone down.

"Maybe the shop would be a good place to **look**," David suggested as they stepped around the corner into the backyard. The door to the shop was open, as usual, and Jonathon walked in. Now this, this was a fascinating place, even if it was messy.

"I've got to get serious about finding this key before **dinner**," Jonathon **said**. "After dinner, I want to play ball with the guys." Jonathon looked around as David stopped to fool with some tools on the workbench. Jonathon didn't see any keys on the workbench. He walked over to look at the pegboard, and sure enough, a key was hanging **there**. Jonathon looked at the key for a minute, studying it.

"It doesn't look like it fits the garage door, but I'll try it to be sure before I take it."

Page 22

1. C or G
2. B
3. F
4. D
5. C or G
6. A
7. E
8. untangle
9. reproduce
10. precaution
11. mislead
12. incomplete
13. biannual
14. tricycle

Page 23

Part 1

1. not correct
2. not logical
3. not formal
4. not dependent
5. not visible
6. not legal
7. not sane
8. not accurate
9. not complete
10. not effective

Part II

1. insecure
2. inaction
3. illegal
4. inexpensive
5. illogical
6. infrequent
7. illegible
8. indirect
9. injustice
10. illiterate

Page 24

Part I

1. misprint
2. misfit
3. misspoke
4. misjudge
5. misspell
6. misplaced
7. misfire
8. misleading
9. mismatch
10. misinformed
11. mistreat
12. misfortune

Part II

1. misunderstood
2. mismatched
3. misbehavior
4. misfortune
5. misspelled
6. mismanaged
7. mislabel

Answer Key (cont.)

8. misquote
9. misprint
10. mistake
11. mislead
12. misjudge

Page 25
1. overwhelmed
2. overflowed
3. overslept
4. overweight
5. overlap
6. overpass
7. overseas
8. overboard
9. overlooked
10. overgrown
11. overcooked
12. overdue

Page 26
Part I
1. material used to carpet a floor
2. materials used to create light
3. material used to cover a roof
4. material used to stuff (a turkey, etc.)
5. material used to clothe a body
6. materials used to make a bed (pillows, sheets, blankets)
7. material used to tile walls or floors
8. material used to cover the legs
9. material used to side a house, barn, or building
10. material used to style hair
11. material used to cover a floor
12. material used to frost (a cake, etc.)

Part II
used in a house:
carpeting   tiling
lighting   flooring
roofing   siding
bedding
something you eat:
salad dressing

stuffing
frosting
used on a body:
clothing
styling gel
leggings

Page 27
1. burning; 5; admitting
2. breaking; 4; amazing
3. feeling; 9; begging
4. giving; 10; breaking
5. exciting; 8; burning
6. shining; 13; diving
7. diving; 6; dying
8. amazing; 2; exciting
9. admitting; 1; feeling
10. winning; 15; giving
11. grabbing; 11; grabbing
12. begging; 3; lying
13. tying; 14; shining
14. dying; 7; tying
15. lying; 12; winning

Page 28
Part I
1. marvelous
2. continuous
3. dangerous
4. courageous
5. miraculous
6. poisonous
7. humorous
8. glamorous
9. famous
10. hazardous

Part II
1. gorgeous
2. famous
3. numerous
4. dangerous
5. courteous
6. poisonous
7. marvelous
8. joyous
9. enormous
10. courageous
11. horrendous
12. humorous

Page 29
Part I
1. attention
2. invention
3. pollution
4. direction

5. revolution
6. reflection
7. explanation
8. completion
9. determination
10. protection
11. reaction
12. quotation
13. repetition
14. prevention
15. combination
16. exclamation

Part II
drop final letter, add *-tion*:
attention
pollution
completion
drop final letter, add vowel + *-tion*:
determination
quotation
combination
change base word + *-tion*:
motion
revolution
explanation
repetition
exclamation

Page 30
Part I
1. confession
2. inclusion
3. television
4. discussion
5. admission
6. comprehension
7. profession
8. extension
9. invasion
10. conclusion

Part II
1. decide
2. divide
3. exclude
4. conclude
5. explode
6. revise
7. invade
8. tense
9. confuse
10. permit

Page 31
1. bor´ -row
2. at´ -tic
3. ban´ -ner
4. bliz´ -zard
5. ef-fect´
6. flut´ -ter
7. hob´ -by
8. let´ -tuce
9. mit´ -ten
10. stal´ -lion
11. soc´ -cer
12. pat´ -tern
13. stub´ -born
14. puz´ -zle
15. lad´ -der
16. fol´ -low
17. but´ -ter

Page 32
1. ache—dull pain; soreness
2. argue—disagree; quarrel
3. bulge—puff up; balloon
4. check—examine; inspect
5. earnest—serious; grave
6. flutter—flap; beat
7. hesitate—pause; delay
8. jealous—envious; covetous
9. locate—find; discover
10. murmur—whisper; mutter
11. object—thing/something; protest
12. perform—play; fulfill
13. prance—leap; spring; jump
14. scamper—run; dart
15. tilt—slant; slope

Page 33
1. F   9. K
2. I   10. M
3. G   11. O
4. D   12. C
5. E   13. B
6. H   14. J
7. L   15. N
8. A

Answer Key *(cont.)*

Page 34
1. cars
2. desks
3. houses
4. trees
5. boys
6. boxes
7. churches
8. dishes
9. dresses
10. waltzes
11. sketches
12. lenses
13. taxes
14. businesses
15. glasses

Page 35
1. bushes; sh; es
2. friends; d; s
3. potatoes; o; es
4. dishes; sh; es
5. minutes; e; s
6. sentences; e; s
7. sandwiches; ch; es
8. addresses; s; es
9. mosquitoes; o; es
10. branches; ch; es
11. weddings; g; s
12. boxes; x; es
13. answers; r; s
14. buses; s; es
15. glasses; s; es

Page 36
1. tale   10. towed
2. hear   11. meet
3. wood   12. mane
4. pour   13. steel
5. tail   14. weak
6. here   15. meddle
7. poor   16. rode
8. would   17. mail
9. stare   18. flour

Page 37
1. trash can   4. rooster
2. brush   5. slowly
3. forget

Page 38
1. cows
2. hard to please
3. one who gives unwanted advice
4. rejoiced, showed joy

Page 43
Possible Answers
I predict Julia will write about what "plantain" is. Julia says, "Have you ever heard of plantain?" Then she says she guesses we don't, and she wants to tell us more about Belize.
I predict Julia will write about the schools. Julia says she has visited schools in Belize, and she probably thinks we are interested in them.

Page 44
Possible Answers
Facts from the story: She entered her office. She put down her briefcase. She had phone messages from people. She took notes as she talked to people on the phone. She called people and asked them questions. She typed up her notes from talking to the people. She said, "Now that's news!" She said, "This'll be great for the front page!"
Conclusion/Inference: Lena is a journalist for a newspaper.

Page 47
b

Page 48
a

Page 49
1. a   3. b
2. b   4. c

Page 50
1. c   3. c
2. a   4. a

Page 51
1. b   3. c
2. b   4. c

Page 52
1. a   3. b
2. c   4. c

Page 53
1. b   3. a
2. a   4. c

Page 54
1. c   3. c
2. b   4. a

Page 55
1. b   3. a
2. c   4. b

Page 57
1. d   4. d
2. b   5. b
3. b

Page 59
1. b   4. b
2. b   5. c
3. b

Page 61
1. a   4. c
2. d   5. b
3. d

Page 63
1. b   4. d
2. d   5. a
3. a

Page 65
1. b   4. a
2. c   5. d
3. d

Page 67
1. D   9. E
2. IT   10. D
3. E   11. D
4. IP   12. D
5. IT   13. E
6. D   14. D
7. D   15. IT
8. E

Page 68
1. school
2. dog
3. sun
4. First graders
5. Spring
Remaining answers will vary.

Page 69
Subject:
2. Everyone
3. Erika

4. cat
5. They
6. She
7. Summer
Predicate:
was laughing.
has a cold.
jumped off the log.
ate the birthday cake.
can do a backwards flip.
is the time for fishing.
Remaining answers will vary.

Page 72
1. excited   4. worried
2. sad   5. happy
3. funny

Page 73
Voices are from the following individuals. Your students will present a wide variety of answers. Accept reasonable responses.
1. 82-year-old female, retired librarian (permission granted by Helen Lantis, April 2000)
2. 15-year-old female, student (permission granted by Amber Mullins, April 2000)
3. 11-year-old male, student (permission granted by Kenneth Mabry, April 2000)

Page 77
There are many ways to travel. People can travel by plane, boat, or train. Cars and buses are other ways to travel. Bicycles, tricycles, scooters, and skateboards are good for getting around. A fun way to travel is on a horse or a donkey. Some people can even travel in a spaceship!

Page 98
1. 17   6. 20
2. 37   7. 27
3. 39   8. 18
4. 91   9. 42
5. 12   10. 25

Answer Key *(cont.)*

11. 7
12. 14
13. 23   19 79
14. 22   20. 51
15. 9   21. 33
16. 36   22. 40
17. 50   23. 14
18. 36   24. 7

Page 99
a. 49 + 57 = $106
b. 26 + 32 = $58
c. 17 + 64 = $81
d. 32 + 57 = $89
e. 64 + 17 + 49 = $130
f. 26 + 57 + 32 = $115

Page 100
1. 83 + 24 + 16 = 123
2. 47 + 21 + 33 = 101
3. 14 + 32 + 24 = 70
4. 36 + 42 + 87 = 165

Page 101
1. 9,312   6. 10,904
2. 12,684   7. 16,866
3. 4,902   8. 10,192
4. 2,956   9. 13,324
5. 17,426   10. 12,129

Cartoon: Steamboat Willie

Page 102
1. $19.35
2. $18.52
3. $15.73
4. $15.76
5. $13.69
6. $14.94

Page 103
1. 22   4. 15
2. 17   5. 45
3. 35   6. 39

Page 104
1. 622   6. 961
2. 396   7. horses
3. 111   8. pigs
4. 621   9. chickens
5. 454   10. more
          horses

Page 105
1. 66,757
2. 45,883
3. 994,888
4. 899,881
5. 192
6. $38,700

Page 106
1. about 100
2. about 500
3. about 100
4. about 800
5. about 400
6. about 400

Page 107
a. 8
b. 33
c. 31
d. 16
e. 62
f. 28
g. 47
h. 6
i. 44
j. 40
k. 72
l. 21
m. 64
n. 31
o. 14
p. 15
q. 4
r. 37
s. 32
t. 64
u. 59
v. 26
w. 5
x. 14

Page 108
a. 93 − 68 = 25
b. 43 − 40 = 3
c. 53 − 28 = 25
d. 83 − 62 = 21

Page 109
Across
1. fourteen
3. nineteen
7. seventeen
9. sixteen
Down
1. fifteen
2. twenty
4. eighteen
5. eleven
6. twelve
8. thirteen

Page 110
1. 35   5. 21
2. 28   6. 30
3. 24   7. 36
4. 27   8. 20

Page 111
1. 72   16. 24
2. 35   17. 30
3. 35   18. 25
4. 77   19. 28
5. 66   20. 72
6. 8   21. 99
7. 0   22. 66
8. 54   23. 60
9. 40   24. 96
10. 0   25. 110
11. 30   26. 54
12. 49   27. 55
13. 40   28. 84
14. 63   29. 72
15. 28

Page 112
1. 60   9. 150
2. 40   10. 120
3. 120   11. 240
4. 72   12. 320
5. 90   13. 280
6. 72   14. 70
7. 56   15. 480
8. 144

Page 113
1. 168   9. 520
2. 357   10. 204
3. 88   11. 392
4. 48   12. 532
5. 384   13. 266
6. 567   14. 699
7. 336   15. 1,869
8. 175

Page 114
1. 258   11. 462
2. 320   12. 783
3. 125   13. 376
4. 245   14. 801
5. 390   15. 112
6. 333   16. 392
7. 528   17. 231
8. 72   18. 891
9. 539   19. 455
10. 279   20. 308

Page 115
1. 18,759   9. 53,504
2. 35,322   10. 69,894
3. 53,656   11. 22,275
4. 2,700   12. 26,862
5. 27,315   13. 18,018
6. 11,856   14. 18,785
7. 10,486   15. 53,754
8. 38,684   16. 25,806

Page 116
1. 16,920   11. 16,000
2. 11,550   12. 27,000
3. 19,260   13. 15,270
4. 3,480   14. 49,560
5. 20,440   15. 56,280
6. 9,510   16. 36,360
7. 16,760   17. 12,900
8. 33,280   18. 26,800
9. 40,000   19. 39,200
10. 36,000 20. 36,000

Page 117
1. 1,537   10. 3,591
2. 2,242   11. 1,452
3. 1,904   12. 1,411
4. 1,387   13. 2,940
5. 5,481   14. 6,080
6. 3,588   15. 3,540
7. 2,436   16. 580
8. 5,022   17. 4,185
9. 891   18. 3,042

Page 118

7	9	8	2	16	5	1
8	5	4	20	3	7	15
56	45	32	43	9	6	11
21	9	50	8	9	5	3
7	3	21	12	81	30	2
4	9	54	7	6	42	2
18	27	20	39	4	8	16

Page 119
Square #1
Top Row: 7
Middle Row: 6, 30
Bottom Row: 35
Square #2
Top Row: 2
Middle Row: 4, 24
Bottom Row: 12
Square #3
Top Row: 1
Middle Row: 11, 33
Bottom Row: 3

Answer Key (cont.)

Page 120
1. 3, 2, 8
2. 8, 5, 3
3. 4, 5, 9
4. 7, 3, 2
5. 5, 5, 4
6. 2, 9, 6
7. 6, 2, 2
8. 6, 4, 3
9. 3, 6, 9

Page 121
1. 140 min. or 2 hr. 20 min.
2. 135 min. or 2 hr. 15 min.
3. 360 min. or 6 hr. 0 min.
4. 100 min. or 1 hr. 40 min.
5. 140 min. or 2 hr. 20 min.
6. 120 min. or 2 hr. 0 min.

Page 122
1. 9
2. 7
3. 5
4. 9
5. 8
6. 7
7. 7
8. 9
9. 7
10. 9
11. 5
12. 4
13. 12
14. 12
15. 7
16. 11
17. 7
18. 9
19. 9
20. 9
21. 5
22. 4
23. 5
24. 6
25. 7
26. 6
27. 7
28. 8

Page 123
1. 5 R1
2. 7 R1
3. 3 R1
4. 5 R1
5. 3 R1
6. 6 R1
7. 9 R1
8. 8 R1
9. 8 R1
10. 8 R1
11. 9 R1
12. 9 R1
13. 4 R3
14. 4 R3
15. 6 R3
16. 5 R4
17. 4 R5
18. 3 R4
19. 9 R4
20. 5 R7
21. 9 R3
22. 6 R7
23. 7 R6
24. 4 R6

Page 124
1. 91
2. 181
3. 314
4. 413
5. 232
6. 384
7. 259
8. 154
9. 462
10. 3,662
11. 2,186
12. 498
13. 1,413
14. 1,679
15. 2,246
16. 859

Page 125
1. 34
2. 21
3. 22
4. 29
5. 24
6. 23
7. 42
8. 11
9. 21
10. 11
11. 32
12. 16

Page 126
1. 56
2. 88
3. 34
4. 90
5. 167
6. 129
7. 8
8. 5
9. 3
10. 566
11. 939
12. 30
13. 1,751
14. 1,414
15. 1,416
16. 46

Page 127
1. 4 R10
2. 9 R10
3. 2 R30
4. 6 R10
5. 4 R30
6. 6 R10
7. 3 R10
8. 5 R10
9. 9 R30
10. 2 R30
11. 4 R50
12. 10 R50
13. 8 R20
14. 6 R20
15. 27 R10
16. 6 R10

Page 128
1. $.99
2. $.71
3. $.71
4. $4.40
5. $.36
6. $1.53
7. $1.20
8. $1.78
9. $.59
10. $1.21
11. $1.04
12. $2.23
13. $17.67
14. $11.02
15. $9.79
16. $5.47

Page 129
1. 7
2. 21
3. 17
4. 23
5. 37
6. 20
7. 20
8. 7
9. 9
10. 12
11. 44
12. 35
13. 125
14. 46
15. 355
16. 441

Page 130

Page 131
Square #1
Top Row: 16
Middle Row: 8, 2
Bottom Row: 4
Square #2
Top Row: 40
Middle Row: 60, 3
Bottom Row: 2
Square #3
Top Row: 50
Middle Row: 40, 4
Bottom Row: 5

Page 132
Martians who landed in the garden said "Take me to your weeder."

Page 133
1. 1/3
2. 1/4
3. 5/6
4. 3/5
5. 7/10
6. 2/6 or 1/3
7. 3/4
8. 1/2

Page 134
1. 1/3
2. 4/6 or 2/3
3. 2/5
4. 3/4
5. 1/2
6. 1/2
7. 5/9
8. 1/4
9. 3/4
10. 3/6 or 1/2
11. 2/4 or 1/2
12. 2/3

Page 135
order: 1/2, 1/3, 1/4, 1/5, 1/6, 1/7, 1/8, 1/9, 1/10

Page 136
1. 1/2
2. 1/7
3. 1/9
4. 5
5. 3
6. 1/6
7. 1/3
8. 1/1
9. 8
10. 6

Page 137
1. A
2. A
3. A
4. D
5. B
6. B
7. A
8. D

Page 138
1. D
2. B
3. D
4. C
5. B
6. C

Page 139
1. D
2. C
3. A
4. D
5. A
6. B
7. B
8. A

Page 140
1. 6/7
2. 4/5
3. 7/12
4. 7/8
5. 7/9
6. 11/14
7. 3/5
8. 11/17
9. 1/3
10. 7/13
11. 7/8
12. 15/19
13. 3/4
14. 13/16
15. 1
16. 7/10

Page 141
1. 1/12
2. 5/8
3. 3/8
4. 1/3
5. 2/3
6. 0
7. 4/5
8. 3/8
9. 1/2
10. 1/5
11. 8/11
12. 3/5
13. 1/10
14. 1/4
15. 1/3
16. 1/14

Page 142
1. 1/8
2. 1/6
3. 5/7
4. 1 1/3
5. 1 1/4
6. 3/7
7. 3/8
8. 1/4
9. 2/4 or 1/2
10. 2/6 or 1/3

Answer Key (cont.)

Page 143
1. 2 1/2
2. 1 1/3
3. 3 1/4
4. 2 2/5
5. 1 1/6
6. 1 1/9
7. 1 2/7
8. 1 1/3
9. 1 3/7
10. 1 3/5
11. 2 1/4
12. 1 1/2
13. 1 2/3
14. 2 1/2
15. 1 5/9
16. 2 2/3
17. 1 3/4
18. 3 2/3
19. 1 1/3
20. 1 8/9

Page 144

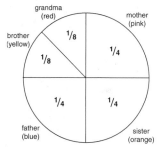

grandma (red) — 1/8
mother (pink) — 1/4
brother (yellow) — 1/8
father (blue) — 1/4
sister (orange) — 1/4

Page 145
1. 4/7
2. 1/6
3. 3/10
4. 3/8
5. 1/3
6. 5/12
7. 2/5
8. 1/2

Page 146
I wanted to own a bakery but I couldn't raise the dough.

Page 147
One more crack like that and I will have to plaster you.

Page 148
1. square matched to cube; triangle matched to triangular pyramid; circle matched to sphere; rectangle matched to rectangular prism
2. rectangle and square
3. triangle and rectangle
4. square
5. circle
6. circle
7. triangle

Page 149
1. octagon
2. pentagon
3. hexagon
4. heptagon
5. decagon
6. nonagon
7. hexagon
8. heptagon
9. decagon

Page 150
1. 6, 0, 12, 8
2. 5, 0, 8, 5
3. 2, 1, 2, 0
4. 1, 1, 1, 1
5. 6, 0, 12, 8
6. 0, 1, 0, 0
7. 7, 0, 15, 10
8. 8, 0, 18, 12
9. 4, 0, 6, 4

Page 151
1. cube
2. rectangular pyramid
3. rectangular prism
4. triangular pyramid
5. cone
6. cylinder

Page 152
1. no
2. no
3. yes
4. yes
5. no
6. yes
7. no
8. no
9.–20. Check to make sure that the student has correctly drawn the line of symmetry on each shape.

Page 153
1. arrow and pentagon
2. hexagon
3. octagon and star
4. square and pentagon
5. triangle
6. rectangle
7. diamond and pentagon

Page 154
1. Congruent
2. Similar
3. Congruent
4. Similar
5. Congruent
6. Similar
7. Congruent
8. Similar
9. Congruent
10. Congruent
11. Similar
12. Congruent
13. Similar
14. Similar
15. Congruent

Page 155
1. 4, 4
2. 3, 3
3. 5, 5
4. 10, 10
5. 4, 4
6. 6, 6
7. 10, 10
8. 6, 6
9. 8, 8
Sample answers:
10. They are the same number.
11. I cannot because there are always the same number of angles as sides.

Page 156
1. Circle the triangle, trapezoid, and cross.
2. right angle
3. acute angle
4. obtuse angle
5. obtuse angle
6. right angle
7. acute angle

Page 157
1. right angle
2. acute angle
3. acute angle
4. obtuse angle
5. obtuse angle
6. right angle
7. right angle
8. obtuse angle
9. obtuse angle
10. right angle
11. obtuse angle
12. right angle

Page 158
1. 0, scalene
2. 2, isosceles
3. 3, equilateral
4. 0, scalene
5. 3, equilateral
6. 2, isosceles

Page 159
1. parallel
2. intersecting
3. parallel
4. parallel
5. parallel
6. intersecting
7. intersecting
8. parallel
9. intersecting
10.–11. Check to make sure the student has drawn the lines correctly.

Page 160
1. $\overleftrightarrow{EF}$
2. $\overleftrightarrow{AB}$
3. $\overleftrightarrow{AB}$
4. $\overleftrightarrow{IJ}$
5. $\overleftrightarrow{GH}$ or $\overleftrightarrow{IJ}$
6. $\overleftrightarrow{KL}$

7. Draw MN parallel to OP.

8. Draw QR intersecting ST.

9. Draw UV parallel to WX. Draw YZ intersecting UV and WX.

10. Draw AB intersecting CD. Draw EF parallel to CD.

Page 161
1. 18 cm
2. 22 cm
3. 14 in.
4. 28 in.
5. 42 mm
6. 56 mm
7. 22 cm
8. 38 cm
9. 28 in.

Page 162
1. 8 in.
2. 14 in.
3. 13 in.
4. 10 ft.
5. 15 ft.
6. 12 ft.
7. 12 yd.
8. 19 yd.
9. 14 yd.
10. 12 in.
11. 12 ft.
12. 20 yd.

Page 163
1. B and E
2. C
3. A
4. D

Page 164
1. 3 x 3 = 9 sq. in.
2. 7 x 1 = 7 sq. in.
3. 5 x 5 = 25 sq. in.
4. 4 x 3 = 12 sq. in.
5. 3 x 1 = 3 sq. ft.

Answer Key *(cont.)*

6. 7 x 7 = 49 sq. ft.
7. 6 inches x 6 inches
8. Possible answers:
   2 inches x 20 inches,
   4 inches x 10 inches,
   8 inches x 5 inches
   40 inches x 1 inch
9. rectangle, 10 inches x
   5 inches, 25 in. x 2 in.
   or 50 in. x 1 in.

Page 165
1. 9 sq. in.
2. 4 sq. in.
3. 1 sq. in.
4. 10 sq. in.
5. 20 sq. in.
6. 18 sq. in.

Sample answers:
7. base of 6 in., height of 4 in.
8. base of 6 in., height of 5 in.

Page 166
1. s = 3 cm

3 x 3 x 3 = 27 cu. cm
2. l = 5 cm, w = 2 cm, h = 3 cm

5 x 2 x 3 = 30 cu. cm
3. l = 5 cm, w = 2 cm, h = 1 cm

5 x 2 x 1 = 10 cu. cm
4. s = 5 cm

5 x 5 x 5 = 125 cu. cm

Page 167
1. radius
2. center
3. diameter
4. radius
5. diameter
6. circumference
7. 6 in.
8. 8 in.
9. 4 in.
10. 4 in.
11. 5 in.
12. 3 in.

Page 168
1. Slide
2. Flip
3. Flip
4. Flip
5. Slide
6. Flip
7. Flip
8. Slide
9. Flip
10. first car
11. second stadium
12. first dog
13. first alien

Page 169
1. 90°   9. 180°
2. 180°   10. 90°
3. 360°   11. 180°
4. 360°   12. 270°
5. 180°   13. 360°
6. 270°   14. 180°
7. 180°   15. 90°
8. 360°

Page 170
You might find it easier to understand each of the graphics on this page if you reproduced them on the board in a much larger size.

Page 171
1. 6   7. |||| |
2. 16   8. |||| ||||
3. 9   9. |||| ||
4. 21   10. |||| |||| |||
5. 10   11. |||| ||||
6. 4   12. |||| |||| |||| ||

Page 172
1. Sunday, 70 fish
2. Friday
3. Tuesday
4. yes – 20 fish
5. 120 fish

Page 173
1. 5 pianos, 10 flutes, 30 guitars, 15 drums, 5 trumpets
2. 25, 20, 15, 25
3. Accept any reasonable explanation.

Page 174
1. watermelon
2. grapes
3. watermelon, peaches, plums, apricots, grapes
4. watermelon 1/2, peaches 1/4, plums 1/8

Page 175
1. 40 animals
2. tigers
3. python, seal
4. horses
5. probably dogs, possibly horses

Page 176
1. homework: 30 minutes; snack: 5 minutes; clothes: 5 minutes; video game: 10 minutes; walking the dog: 10 minutes
2. Answers will vary. Check as a class exercise.

Page 177
No key needed

Page 178
1. K A.M.: 20 K P.M.: 10
   1st: 60
   2nd: 80
   3rd: 55
   4th: 50
   5th: 35
   6th: 20
2. 2nd grade
3. K A.M. and 6th grade

Page 179

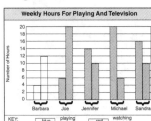

Page 180
1. week 1: 0, week 2:2, week 3:2, week 4:4, week 5:3 week, 6:5
2. week 6
3. week 1
4. last few weeks

Page 181
1. Wednesday
2. 220 minutes
3. 4 days
1. Hoopers
2. Dunkers
3. Dunkers

Page 182
1. a. 1
    b. 8
    c. 5
    d. 4
    e. 3
    f. 7
2. weather-related answers: school-related answers

Page 183

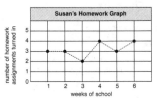

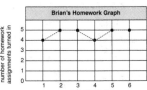

Page 184
A new bicycle

Page 185
#1 = M, #2 = W, #3 = V

Page 186
1. 10:15 – 11:45
2. calendar, music, lunch
3. sharing, reading, writing, math, science, art, recess

Page 187
1. teepee
2. bow and arrow
3. glass beads
4. land
5. nomads
6. sign language
7. buffalo
8. horse
9. long house
10. mesa
11. salmon
12. moccasin
13. maize
14. potlatch
15. squash
Bonus: treaty

Answer Key (cont.)

Page 188
1. bowstrings
2. scouts
3. parfleches
4. wolf skin
5. arrows
6. blankets
7. corral
Down: buffalo

Page 189
1. The Spaniards
2. big dogs
3. Southwest
4. 16th century
5. Horses allowed Native Americans to travel faster, carry heavier loads and hunt more easily.
6. by raiding Spanish settlements

Page 190
1. a; 2. b; 3. b; 4. c

Page 191
1. b; 2. c; 3. a; 4. b

Page 192
Area:
1. RI
2. DE
3. CT
4. NJ
5. NH
6. MA
7. MD
8. SC
9. VA
10. PA
11. NC
12. NY
13. GA

Population:
1. DE
2. RI
3. NH
4. CT
5. SC
6. MD
7. MA
8. VA
9. NC
10. GA
11. NJ
12. PA
13. NY

Page 193
1. Have you something to do tomorrow, do it today.
2. A true friend is the best possession.
3. No gain, without pain.
4. Be always ashamed to catch thyself idle.
5. People who are wrapped up in themselves make small packages.
6. A penny saved is a penny earned.
7. Early to bed and early to rise, makes a man healthy, wealthy, and wise.
8. 'Tis easier to prevent bad habits than to break them.
9. An ounce of prevention is worth a pound of cure.
10. A bird in hand is worth two in the bush.

Page 194
1. "A house divided against itself cannot stand."
2. "Fair play is a jewel."
3. "Work, work, work is the main thing."
4. "Four score and seven years ago…"

Page 195
1. ground
2. flag
3. vertically
4. torn
5. destroyed
6. flag
Old Glory

Page 197
1. 11,100,000; 11,000,000
2. a. 9%
   b. 6.4% (or 6%)
   c. 4.5% (or 5%)
3. 12.7%

Page 198
1. Robert Cavelier
2. Hernando Cortes
3. Juan Ponce de Leon
4. Bartolomeu Dias
5. Christopher Columbus
6. Samuel de Champlain
7. Henry Hudson
8. Jacques Cartier
9. Francisco Pizarro
10. Ferdinand Magellan

Page 199
1. answers will vary
2. the Atlantic and the Pacific Oceans
3. the Arctic Ocean
4. the Indian Ocean
5. the Atlantic Ocean
6. South America

Page 201
1. one
2. train track
3. southeast
4. four
5. two
6. three
7. southwest
8. by train
9. Riverside
10. one

Page 202
1. Grand Junction
2. Sterling
3. Denver
4. Lamar
5. Durango
6. Colorado Springs
7. Glenwood Springs
8. Campo
9. Craig
10. Kanorado

Page 204
1. Europe
2. South America
3. car
4. the Pacific Ocean
5. Africa
6. the Indian Ocean
7. Asia
8. Australia
9. boat
10. the Arctic Ocean
11. Antarctica
12. the Atlantic Ocean

Page 205
1. *Hemisphere* means half of a ball or globe.
2. the equator
3.–5. Answers will vary.
6. South America and Antarctica
7. the Northern Hemisphere
8. South America

Page 206
1. Northern and Eastern
2. three (Northern, Southern, and Western)
3. Antarctica and Australia
4. Answers will vary.
5. South America, Africa, Antarctica, Australia
6. North America
7. Atlantic Ocean, Pacific Ocean, Arctic Ocean
8. four

Page 207
1. lines of latitude
2. lines of longitude
3. They are used for locating places on the globe/Earth.
4. the equator
5. the prime meridian

Page 208
1. 35 and 40
2. 27
3. Wayne
4. Glen Ridge, 33
5. a. 15
   b. 37
   c. 27
   d. 48

Page 209
1. south and east
2. Ekalaka
3. Boyes, Hammond, Alzada
4. Boxelder Creek
5. Medicine Rocks

Page 210
1. Saskatchewan and Ontario
2. Yukon Territory Nunavut, and Northwest Territory
3. rainy and cloudy
4. Quebec
5. sunny
6. cloudy

Page 211
nuts, apple, celery, cheese, carrot, grapes, orange, bread, pear, tomato

Answer Key *(cont.)*

Page 212
1. dairy
2. fruits
3. meat & fish
4. bread & pasta
5. fats & sweets

Page 213
1. broccoli
2. pumpkin
3. spaghetti
4. yogurt
5. vegetable

Page 214

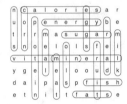

Bonus: a really good appetite

Page 215
"An apple a day keeps the doctor away."

Page 216
1. butter
2. soap
3. ink
4. cereal
5. plastics
6. paper
7. bleach
8. milk
9. dyes
10. candy
11. meat sauce
12. dried coffee

Page 217
1. skeletal
2. xray
3. nervous
4. circulatory
5. endocrine
6. respiratory
7. muscular
8. digestive

Page 218
1. midbrain
2. pons.
3. medula
4. cerebrum
5. cerebellum
6. spinal cord

Page 219
A=312	Z=926
E=176	C=12
I=213	G=21
M=75	K=13
Q=156	O=14
U=186	S=32
Y=820	W=23
B=637	D=201
F=111	H=49
J=90	L=92
N=96	P=444
R=760	T=499
V=626	X=91

1. caldera
2. seismometer
3. volcanology
4. eruptions
5. magma
6. planets
7. Explosive
8. Pyroclastic
9. Mudflows
10. pumice

Page 220
1. b
2. c
3. a
4. b

Page 221
1. c
2. b
3. a
4. b

Page 222
1. crust
2. California
3. fault
4. plate
5. earthquake
6. rock
7. moving
8. shakes

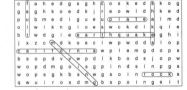

Page 223
1. 1895
2. 1975
3. 2,000
4. 120
5. 15
6. 20
7. 1,000
8. 437
9. 15

Page 224

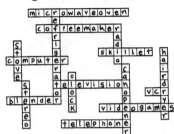

Page 225

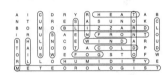

Bonus: dry, sun, wet

Page 226
1. snow
2. mild or dew
3. thunder
4. sun
5. rain or rained
6. cloud
7. season
8. cold
9. wind
10. ice

Page 227
1. b
2. a
3. c
4. b

Page 228
1. moon
2. Mars
3. solar system
4. satellite
5. Saturn
6. Venus
7. temperature
8. asteroid
9. Mercury
10. Jupiter

11. atmosphere
12. distance
13 space
14. meteor
15. Neptune
16. planet
17. Uranus
18. Pluto
19. comet
20 Earth

Page 229
1. Earth
2. endangered
3. environment
4. landfill
5. smog
6. recycle
7. extinct
8. preserve
9. green
10. organic
11. food chain
12. habitat
13. water
14. air
15. food web
16. pollution
17. waste
18. trash
19. dump
20. rain forest

Page 230

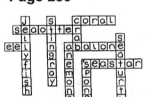